mommy & me
crocheted hats

0 11557 01327 6

mommy & me
crocheted hats

Kristi Simpson

STACKPOLE
BOOKS

Published by
STACKPOLE BOOKS
5067 Ritter Road
Mechanicsburg, PA 17055
www.stackpolebooks.com

Printed in U.S.A.

10 9 8 7 6 5 4 3 2 1

First edition

Cover design by Caroline Stover

Library of Congress Cataloging-in-Publication Data

Simpson, Kristi.
  Mommy & me crocheted hats : 30 silly, sweet & fun hats for kids of all ages / Kristi Simpson. — First edition.
    pages cm
  ISBN 978-0-8117-1327-6
  1. Crocheting—Patterns. 2. Hats. I. Title. II. Title: Mommy and me crocheted hats.
  TT825.S5463 2014
  746.43'4—dc23
                              2013041545

Contents

Acknowledgments vi
Introduction 1

Mary Kate Cloche   2   Daddy's Bearded Dude Beanie   60

Horse Hat   6   Luvbug Slouchy   64

Giggle Monster   10   Sweetheart Sunhat   68

Ahoy Matey! Pirate Hat   14   Lamb Bonnet   72

Bubblegum Machine Beanie   18   Just Like Mommy Ribbed Beanie   76

Downtown Girl Slouchy   22   Basketweave Beanie   80

Rosey Newsboy   24   Buddy Bobbles   84

Giggles and Curls Hat   28   Winter Lodge Hat   88

Baby Doll Hat   32   Hooded Scarf   92

Zack the Zombie   36   Sassy Girl   96

Twisted Stitches Beanie   40   You Have My Heart Beanie   100

I'm an Elf! Pixie   44   Snowman Hat   104

Sock Monkey Twist   48   Gone Huntin' Camo Cap   108

Groovy Waves Beanie   52   Pigtail Hat   112

Ocean Air Cloche   56   Thick and Thin Hat   116

How to Read My Patterns 120
Stitch Guide 122
Finishing Touches 133
Visual Index 136

Acknowledgments

I would like to thank all of the parents and grandparents who participated in the photography sessions for this book. Thanks to you, this book is filled with smiles and giggles that will delight everyone who sees them!

Also, I must give many thanks to Pam Hoenig, my editor, for her hard work; to the Stackpole team for their professionalism; and to my team of testers, Ashley Scott and Ashlee Young, for their outstanding assistance. Ashley Scott, also my photo editor, deserves a million thanks for her hard work.

Finally, my family is my inspiration for each and every design: my husband, Jason, and our children, Jacob, Kimberly, Allison, James, and Ryan. You bring so much love and laughter to my life and to our family!

Introduction

My very first design ever was a hat, and they continue to be a sweet spot for me as a designer. You can go in so many directions when creating a new hat—silly, sweet, functional, fashionable. The designs in this book are perfect for kids of all ages, no matter the style you're looking for. As I worked up the patterns, I had my five-year-old twins in mind, but when my teenagers started grabbing the hats hot off the crochet hook, I knew I had a hit!

And even though the title of this collection is *Mommy & Me Crocheted Hats,* you don't have to be a mom (or dad) to make them. These caps, cloches, beanies, slouchies, and other toppers are perfect gifts for new moms and dads, nieces and nephews, brothers and sisters. Crochet up a pair to wear with your own mom or dad, or with your best friend or significant other. Or just make them one at a time. No matter which you pick, the patterns are simple to follow and guaranteed to bring smiles.

If you're a beginner at crochet, hats are a great place to start. I would particularly suggest you try the Ahoy Matey! Pirate Hat (page 14), Giggle Monster (page 10), Pigtail Hat (page 112), Snowman Hat (page 104), or the Sweetheart Sunhat (page 68). At the back of the book you'll find a Stitch Guide with step-by-step photo tutorials for all the stitches used in these (and all the other) patterns.

As much as I enjoyed creating these designs for you, taking the photographs for the book was as much or even more fun. None of the models are professionals—they are all moms and dads or grandmas and grandpas having a great time in front of the camera with their son, daughter, or grandchild. These hats naturally made them smile and laugh, and I invite you to join in the fun!

Mary Kate Cloche

Τhis classy hat is perfect for all seasons. Dress it up or down and you will have the perfect accessory for you and your sweet girl. The Puff Stitches create a fantastic texture that sets this hat apart.

Skill Level

Intermediate

Finished Measurements

Head circumference: Small: 15–17.5"/38–44.5 cm, Medium: 17.5–19"/44.5–48 cm, Large: 19–22.5"/48–57 cm
Height: Small: 6–6.5"/15–16.5 cm, Medium: 6.5–7"/16.5–18 cm, Large: 7–7.5"/18–19 cm

Yarn

• Red Heart Boutique Unforgettable Yarn, medium worsted weight #4 yarn (100% acrylic; 278 yd/3.5 oz, 256 m/100 g per skein)
    1 skein #E793 Tidal

Hook and Other Materials

• N-13 (9.0 mm) hook or size needed to obtain gauge
• Yarn needle

Gauge

10 sts and 15 rows in sc = 4"/10 cm square

Notes

1. The hat is worked from the top down in rounds.
2. The ch2 or ch1 at the beginning of each round is not counted as a stitch.
3. Be sure to work the puff stitch loosely. Each puff stitch is approximately ³⁄₄" long.

Special Techniques
Puff Stitch

NOTE: The directions here call for 4 yarn overs. When the pattern calls for "Puff-5 Stitch," simply repeat step 4, for a total of 5 yarn overs and 11 loops on the hook. Then complete step 5.

1 Yarn over, insert hook into stitch, yarn over, and pull yarn back through: 3 loops on hook.

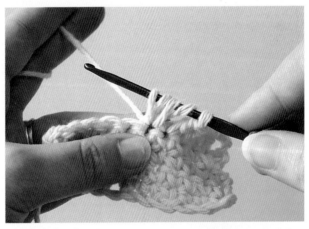

2 Yarn over, insert hook into SAME stitch, yarn over, and pull yarn back through: 5 loops on hook.

(continued)

3 Yarn over, insert hook into SAME stitch, yarn over, and pull yarn back through: 7 loops on hook.

4 Yarn over, insert hook into SAME stitch, yarn over, and pull yarn back through: 9 loops on hook.

5 Yarn over, pull yarn through all loops on hook to complete the stitch.

Hat

SMALL

Ch4, sl st to first chain to create a ring.

Round 1: Ch2, 10 Puff Stitches (see Special Technique) in ring, sl st to first stitch to join (10 sts).

Round 2: Ch2, * (Puff Stitch, ch1) in each stitch, sl st to first stitch to join (20 sts).

Round 3: Ch2, * (Puff Stitch, ch1, Puff Stitch) in next Puff Stitch, repeat from * to complete round, sl st to first stitch to join (30 sts).

Round 4: Ch2, * (Puff Stitch, ch2, Puff Stitch) in each ch1 space, repeat from * to complete round, sl st to first stitch to join (40 sts).

Round 5: Ch2, * (Puff-5 Stitch, ch3, Puff-5 Stitch) in each ch2 space, repeat from * to complete round, sl st to first stitch to join (50 sts).

Round 6: Ch2, * (Puff-5 Stitch, ch3, Puff-5 Stitch) in each ch3 space, repeat from * to complete round, sl st to first stitch to join.

Rounds 7–9: Repeat Round 6.

Rounds 10–12: Ch1, sc in each stitch, sl st to first stitch to join.

Fasten off. Weave in ends.

MEDIUM

Ch4, sl st to first chain to create a ring.

Round 1: Ch2, 11 Puff Stitches (see Special Technique) in ring, sl st to first stitch to join (11 sts).

Round 2: Ch2, * (Puff Stitch, ch1) in each stitch, sl st to first stitch to join (22 sts).

Round 3: Ch2, * (Puff Stitch, ch1, Puff Stitch) in next Puff Stitch, repeat from * to complete round, sl st to first stitch to join (33 sts).

Round 4: Ch2, * (Puff Stitch, ch2, Puff Stitch) in each ch1 space, repeat from * to complete round, sl st to first stitch to join (44 sts).

Round 5: Ch2, * (Puff-5 Stitch, ch3, Puff-5 Stitch) in each ch2 space, repeat from * to complete round, sl st to first stitch to join (55 sts).

Round 6: Ch2, * (Puff-5 Stitch, ch3, Puff-5 Stitch) in each ch3 space, repeat from * to complete round, sl st to first stitch to join.

Rounds 7–10: Repeat Round 6.

Rounds 11–13: Ch1, sc in each stitch, sl st to first stitch to join.

Fasten off. Weave in ends.

LARGE

Ch4, sl st to first chain to create a ring.

Round 1: Ch2, 10 Puff Stitches (see Special Technique) in ring, sl st to first stitch to join (10 sts).

Round 2: Ch2, * (Puff Stitch, ch1) in each stitch, sl st to first stitch to join (20 sts).

Round 3: Ch2, * (Puff Stitch, ch1, Puff stitch) in next Puff Stitch, repeat from * to complete round, sl st to first stitch to join (30 sts).

Round 4: Ch2, * (Puff Stitch, ch2, Puff Stitch) in each ch1 space, repeat from * to complete round, sl st to first stitch to join (40 sts).

Round 5: Ch2, * (Puff-5 Stitch, ch3, Puff-5 Stitch) in each ch2 space, repeat from * to complete round, sl st to first stitch to join (50 sts).

Rounds 6–10: Ch3, (Puff-5 Stitch, ch2, Puff-5 Stitch), ch1, * (ch1, Puff-5 Stitch, ch2, Puff-5 Stitch, ch1) in next ch3 space, repeat from * to complete round, sl st to the third chain of first ch3 to join (60 sts).

Rounds 11–13: Ch1, sc in each stitch, sl st to first stitch to join.

Fasten off. Weave in ends.

Horse Hat

S addle up in this perfect horse hat! This adorable topper will "giddy-up" the fun! Great for dress up, playtime, and gift-giving.

Skill Level

Intermediate

Finished Measurements

Head circumference: Small: 15–17.5"/38–44.5 cm, Medium: 17.5–19"/44.5–48 cm, Large: 19–22.5"/48–57 cm
Height: Small: 6–6.5"/15–16.5 cm, Medium: 6.5–7"/16.5–18 cm, Large: 7–7.5"/18–19 cm

Yarn

- I Love This Yarn, medium worsted weight #4 yarn (100% acrylic; 355 yd/7 oz, 325 m/ 198 g per skein)
    1 skein #757 Taupe (Color A)
    1 skein #240 Linen (Color B)

Hook and Other Materials

- H-8 (5.0 mm) hook or size to obtain gauge
- 2 stitch markers
- Yarn needle
- 2 small black buttons
- Sewing thread and needle
- Fiberfill

Gauge

11 sts and 10 rows in dc = 4"/10 cm square

Notes

1. The hat is worked from the top down in rounds.
2. The first ch1 or ch2 of each round does not count as a stitch.
3. The nose and nose stripe are crocheted directly onto the hat after finishing the body of the hat. The ears and nostrils are made separately and sewn on. The fringe is added last.
4. See page 124 for a tutorial on crocheting into the Back Loop Only (blo), page 126 for Single Crochet Decrease (sc dec), and page 128 for Double Crochet Decrease (dc dec).

Hat

SMALL

Using Color A, ch4, sl st to first chain to create a ring.
Round 1: Ch2, (dc, sc) 5 times in ring, sl st to first stitch to join (10 sts).
Round 2: Ch1, (sc, dc) in each stitch, sl st to first stitch to join (20 sts).
Round 3: Ch2, * dc, (sc dc) in next stitch, sc, (dc, sc) in next stitch, repeat from * to complete round, sl st to first stitch to join (30 sts).

Round 4: Ch1, * sc, dc, (sc, dc) in next stitch, repeat from * to complete round, sl st to first stitch to join (40 sts).
Round 5: Ch2, * dc, sc, dc, (sc, dc) in next stitch, sc, dc, sc, (dc, sc) in next stitch, repeat from * to complete round, sl st to first stitch to join (50 sts).
Rounds 6–16: Ch2, * dc, sc, repeat from * to complete round, sl st to first stitch to join.
Fasten off. Weave in ends.

MEDIUM

Using Color A, ch4, sl st to first chain to create a ring.
Round 1: Ch2, (dc, sc) 5 times in ring, sl st to first stitch to join (10 sts).
Round 2: Ch1, (sc, dc) in each stitch, sl st to first stitch to join (20 sts).
Round 3: Ch2, * dc, (sc dc) in next stitch, sc, (dc, sc) in next stitch, repeat from * to complete round, sl st to first stitch to join (30 sts).
Round 4: Ch1, * sc, dc, (sc, dc) in next stitch, repeat from * to complete round, sl st to first stitch to join (40 sts).
Round 5: Ch2, * dc, sc, dc, (sc, dc) in next stitch, sc, dc, sc, (dc, sc) in next stitch, repeat from * to complete round, sl st to first stitch to join (50 sts).
Round 6: Ch1, * sc, dc, sc, dc (sc, dc) in next stitch, repeat from * to complete round, sl st to first stitch to join (60 sts).
Rounds 7–17: Ch2, * dc, sc, repeat from * to complete round, sl st to first stitch to join.
Fasten off. Weave in ends.

LARGE

Using Color A, ch4, sl st to first chain to create a ring.
Round 1: Ch2, (dc, sc) 5 times in ring, sl st to first stitch to join (10 sts).
Round 2: Ch1, (sc, dc) in each stitch, sl st to first stitch to join (20 sts).
Round 3: Ch2, * dc, (sc dc) in next stitch, sc, (dc, sc) in next stitch, repeat from * to complete round, sl st to first stitch to join (30 sts).
Round 4: Ch1, * sc, dc, (sc, dc) in next stitch, repeat from * to complete round, sl st to first stitch to join (40 sts).
Round 5: Ch2, * dc, sc, dc, (sc, dc) in next stitch, sc, dc, sc, (dc, sc) in next stitch, repeat from * to complete round, sl st to first stitch to join (50 sts).
Round 6: Ch1, * sc, dc, sc, dc, (sc, dc) in next stitch, repeat from * to complete round, sl st to first stitch to join (60 sts).
Round 7: Ch2, * dc, sc, dc, sc, dc, (sc, sc) in next stitch, sc, dc, sc, dc, sc, (dc, sc) in next stitch, repeat from * to complete round, sl st to first stitch to join (70 sts).
Rounds 8–18: Ch2, * dc, sc in next stitch, repeat from * to complete round, sl st to first stitch to join.
Fasten off. Weave in ends.

Nose

SMALL

Row 1: Join Color B in any stitch of last round, ch1, sc20 in stitches across last row of hat (20 sts).
Row 2: Turn, ch1, sc in blo of each stitch.
Rows 3–8: Turn, ch1, sc in each stitch.
Row 9: Turn, sc dec twice, sc12, sc dec twice (16 sts).
Row 10: Turn, sc dec twice, sc8, sc dec twice (12 sts).
Row 11: Turn, sc dec twice, sc4, sc dec twice (8 sts).
Fasten off.

MEDIUM

Row 1: Join Color B in any stitch of last round, ch1, sc24 in stitches across last row of hat (24 sts).
Row 2: Turn, ch1, sc in blo of each stitch.
Rows 3–9: Turn, ch1, sc in each stitch.
Row 10: Turn, sc dec twice, sc16, sc dec twice (20 sts).
Row 11: Turn, sc dec twice, sc12, sc dec twice (16 sts).
Row 12: Turn, sc dec twice, sc8, sc dec twice (12 sts).
Fasten off.

LARGE

Row 1: Join Color B in any stitch of last round, ch1, sc26 in stitches across last row of hat (26 sts).
Row 2: Turn, ch1, sc in blo of each stitch.
Rows 3–10: Turn, ch1, sc in each stitch.
Row 11: Turn, sc dec twice, sc18, sc dec twice (22 sts).

Row 12: Turn, sc dec twice, sc14, sc dec twice.
Row 13: Turn, sc dec twice, sc10, sc dec twice.
Fasten off.

NOTE: The completed "nose" will look like a raised flap on the edge of the beanie.

Join yarn at base of hat on bottom right of nose, ch1, sc around nose using ends of rows as stitches. Fasten off, leaving a long tail. Using yarn needle, sew nose onto hat, leaving one edge open. Stuff and shape it with fiberfill. Finish sewing edge of nose. Fasten off. Weave in ends.

Nose Stripe

Locate the center stitch on top of the nose. Join Color B 2 stitches to the right of center st.

SMALL & MEDIUM

Row 1: Ch1, sc5 (5 sts).
Rows 2–18: Turn, ch1, sc in each stitch.
Fasten off.

LARGE

Row 1: Ch1, sc5 (5 sts).
Rows 2–22: Turn, ch1, sc in each stitch.
Fasten off.

Using yarn needle, sew nose stripe onto hat.

Nostrils (make 2)

ALL SIZES

Using Color A, ch2.
Round 1: 6sc in second chain from hook, sl st to first sc to join (6 sts).
Fasten off, leaving a long tail to sew onto nose.

Ears (make 2)

ALL SIZES

Using Color A, ch4.
Round 1: 3dc in fourth chain from hook, sl st to first stitch to join (3 sts).
Round 2: Ch2, 2dc in each stitch, sl st to first stitch to join (6 sts).
Round 3: Ch2, 2dc in each stitch, sl st to first stitch to join (12 sts).
Round 4: Ch2, * dc, 2dc in next stitch, repeat from * to complete round, sl st to first stitch to join (18 sts).
Rounds 5–6: Ch2, dc in each stitch, sl st to first stitch to join.
Round 7: Ch1, * dc, dc dec, repeat from * to complete round, sl st to first stitch to join (12 sts).
Fasten off, leaving a long tail to sew onto hat.
   Fold the end of each ear together and sew to create contour with the yarn needle. Sew the ears onto the hat. Weave in ends.

Mane

Fringe will be added along the last row of the nose stripe, over the top of the hat, and down the last two rows to the back to create the horse's mane.

Cut 50–60 lengths of Color B approximately 12"/30.5 cm long. Using two strands at once, fold the lengths in half, pull the folded center through the last row of the Nose Stripe, and finish by pulling the ends through the loop and pulling tight. In the same way, continue to add the fringe over the top of hat, in between the ears and down the back onto the last two rows. Trim evenly.

Finishing

Using a sewing needle and thread, sew the buttons onto hat on each side of the nose stripe for eyes.
   Using a yarn needle, sew the nostrils onto each side of the nose. Fasten off. Weave in ends.

Giggle Monster

Can you honestly say this hat doesn't make you laugh? Top your li'l monster with this hat and you will have everyone else giggling over the cuteness too!

Skill Level

Beginner

Finished Measurements

Head circumference: X-Small: 12–14.5"/30.5–37 cm, Small: 15–17.5"/38–44.5 cm, Medium: 17.5–19"/44.5–48 cm, Large: 19–22.5"/48–57 cm, X-Large: 23–24.5"/58.5–62 cm
Height: X-Small: 4.5–6"/11.5–15 cm, Small: 6–6.5"/15–16.5 cm, Medium: 6.5–7"/16.5–18 cm, Large: 7–7.5"/18–19 cm, X-Large: 7.5–8"/19–20.5 cm

Yarn

- Lion Brand Pound of Love, medium worsted weight #4 yarn (100% acrylic; 1,020 yd/16 oz, 933 m/454 g per skein)
    1 skein #5728399 Turquoise (Color A)
- Lion Brand Vanna's Choice, medium worsted weight #4 yarn (100% acrylic; 170 yd/3.5 oz, 155 m/100 g per skein)
    1 skein #860-100 White (Color B)
    1 skein #860-140 Dusty Rose (Color C)
    1 skein #860-194 Lime (Color D)
    1 skein #860-135 Rust (Color E)
    1 skein #860-151 Black (Color F)

Hook and Other Materials

- H-8 (5.0 mm) hook or size to obtain gauge
- Yarn needle
- 2 small black buttons
- Sewing needle and thread

Gauge

13 sts and 16 rows in sc = 4"/10 cm square

Notes

1. The hat is worked from the top down in rounds.
2. The ch2 at the beginning of each round does not count as a stitch.
3. For the last round, when you change colors, you will carry the old yarn, instead of fastening it off. That will allow you to simply pick the yarn up later, with no ends to weave in. For a tutorial, see page 132.
4. To change colors, push the hook through the last stitch of the first color, pull the yarn back through, yarn over with the NEXT color, and pull through. Color change is complete. Also see page 131 for a tutorial.
5. You can use any coordinating colors for the monster spikes and trim; I used pink and green for the mom and orange and green for her boy.
6. See page 128 for a tutorial on Double Crochet Decrease (dc dec), page 127 for Half Double Crochet Decrease (hdc dec), and page 126 for Single Crochet Decrease (sc dec).

Hat

X-SMALL

Using Color A, ch4.
Round 1: 10dc in fourth chain from hook, sl st to first stitch to join (10 sts).
Round 2: Ch2, 2hdc in each stitch, sl st to first stitch to join (20 sts).
Round 3: Ch2, * dc, 2dc in next stitch, repeat from * to complete round, sl st to first stitch to join (30 sts).
Round 4: Ch2, * hdc2, 2hdc in next stitch, repeat from * to complete round, sl st to first stitch to join (40 sts).
Round 5: Ch2, dc in each stitch, sl st to first stitch to join.
Round 6: Ch2, hdc in each stitch, sl st to first stitch to join.
Rounds 7–10: Repeat Rows 5–6 twice.
Rounds 11–13: Ch1, sc in each stitch, sl st to first stitch to join.
Round 14: Drop Color A, join Color C and Color D, ch1; changing colors each stitch, sc in each stitch, sl st to first stitch to join.
Fasten off. Weave in ends.

SMALL

Using Color A, ch4.
Round 1: 10dc in fourth chain from hook, sl st to first stitch to join (10 sts).
Round 2: Ch2, 2hdc in each stitch, sl st to first stitch to join (20 sts).
Round 3: Ch2, * dc, 2dc in next stitch, repeat from * to complete round, sl st to first stitch to join (30 sts).
Round 4: Ch2, * hdc2, 2hdc in next stitch, repeat from * to complete round, sl st to first stitch to join (40 sts).
Round 5: Ch2, * dc3, 2dc in next stitch, repeat from * to complete round, sl st to first stitch to join (50 sts).
Round 6: Ch2, hdc in each stitch, sl st to first stitch to join.
Round 7: Ch2, dc in each stitch, sl st to first stitch to join.
Rounds 8–11: Repeat Rounds 6 and 7 twice.
Round 12: Repeat Round 6.
Round 13: Ch2, * hdc3, hdc dec, repeat from * to complete round, sl st to first stitch to join (40 sts).
Rounds 14–16: Ch1, sc in each stitch, sl st to first stitch to join.
Round 17: Drop Color A, join Color C and Color D, ch1; changing colors each stitch, sc in each stitch, sl st to first stitch to join.
Fasten off. Weave in ends.

MEDIUM

Using Color A, ch4.

Round 1: 12dc in fourth chain from hook, sl st to first stitch to join (12 sts).

Round 2: Ch2, 2hdc in each stitch, sl st to first stitch to join (24 sts).

Round 3: Ch2, * dc, 2dc in next stitch, repeat from * to complete round, sl st to first stitch to join (36 sts).

Round 4: Ch2, * hdc2, 2hdc in next stitch, repeat from * to complete round, sl st to first stitch to join (48 sts).

Round 5: Ch2, * dc3, 2dc in next stitch, repeat from * to complete round, sl st to first stitch to join (60 sts).

Round 6: Ch2, hdc in each stitch, sl st to first stitch to join.

Round 7: Ch2, dc in each stitch, sl st to first stitch to join.

Rounds 8–15: Repeat Rounds 6 and 7 three times.

Round 16: Ch2, * hdc3, hdc dec, repeat from * to complete round, sl st to first stitch to join (48 sts).

Rounds 17–19: Ch1, sc in each stitch, sl st to first stitch to join.

Round 20: Drop Color A, join Color C and Color D, ch1; changing colors each stitch, sc in each stitch, sl st to first stitch to join.

Fasten off. Weave in ends.

LARGE

Using Color A, ch4.

Round 1: 11dc in fourth chain from hook, sl st to first stitch to join (11 sts).

Round 2: Ch2, 2hdc in each stitch, sl st to first stitch to join (22 sts).

Round 3: Ch2, * dc, 2dc in next stitch, repeat from * to complete round, sl st to first stitch to join (33 sts).

Round 4: Ch2, * hdc2, 2hdc in next stitch, repeat from * to complete round, sl st to first stitch to join (44 sts).

Round 5: Ch2, * dc3, 2dc in next stitch, repeat from * to complete round, sl st to first stitch to join (55 sts).

Round 6: Ch2, * hdc4, 2hdc in next stitch, repeat from * to complete round, sl st to first stitch to join (66 sts).

Round 7: Ch2, dc in each stitch, sl st to first stitch to join.

Round 8: Ch2, hdc in each stitch, sl st to first stitch to join.

Rounds 9–17: Repeat Rounds 7 and 8 five times.

Round 18: Ch2, * dc4, dc dec, repeat from * to complete round, sl st to first stitch to join (55 sts).

Rounds 19–21: Ch1, sc in each stitch, sl st to first stitch to join.

Round 22: Drop Color A, join Color C and Color D, ch1; changing colors each stitch, sc in each stitch, sl st to first stitch to join.

Fasten off. Weave in ends.

X-LARGE

Using Color A, ch4.
Round 1: 12dc in fourth chain from hook, sl st to first stitch to join (12 sts).
Round 2: Ch2, 2hdc in each stitch, sl st to first stitch to join (24 sts).
Round 3: Ch2, * dc, 2dc in next stitch, repeat from * to complete round, sl st to first stitch to join (36 sts).
Round 4: Ch2, * hdc2, 2hdc in next stitch, repeat from * to complete round, sl st to first stitch to join (48 sts).
Round 5: Ch2, * dc3, 2dc in next stitch, repeat from * to complete round, sl st to first stitch to join (60 sts).
Round 6: Ch2, * hdc4, 2hdc in next stitch, repeat from * to complete round, sl st to first stitch to join (72 sts).
Round 7: Ch2, dc in each stitch, sl st to first stitch to join.
Round 8: Ch2, hdc in each stitch, sl st to first stitch to join.
Rounds 9–17: Repeat Rounds 7 and 8 five times.
Round 18: Ch2, * dc6, dc dec, repeat from * to complete round, sl st to first stitch to join (64 sts).
Rounds 19–21: Ch1, sc in each stitch, sl st to first stitch to join.
Round 22: Drop Color A, join Color C and Color D, ch1; changing colors each stitch, sc in each stitch, sl st to first stitch to join (64 sts).
Fasten off. Weave in ends.

Large Eye

Using Color B, ch2.
Round 1: 6sc in second chain from hook (6 sts).
Round 2: Working continuously in the round, 2sc in each stitch (12 sts).
Round 3: * Sc, 2sc in next stitch, repeat from * to complete round (18 sts).
Round 4: * Sc2, 2sc in next stitch, repeat from * to complete round (24 sts).
Round 5: * Sc3, 2sc in next stitch, repeat from * to complete round (32 sts).
Round 6: * Sc4, 2sc in next stitch, repeat from * to complete round. Sl st to first stitch to join (36 sts).
Fasten off. Weave in ends.

Small Eye

Using Color B, ch2.
Round 1: 6sc in second chain from hook (6 sts).
Round 2: Working continuously in the round, 2sc in each stitch (12 sts).
Round 3: * Sc, 2sc in next stitch, repeat from * to complete round. Sl st to first st to join (18 sts).
Fasten off, leaving a long tail to sew onto hat.

Monster Spikes (make 5 in coordinating colors)

Ch2.
Round 1: 4sc in second chain from hook (4 sts).
Round 2: Working continuously in the round, 2sc in each stitch (8 sts).
Round 3: * Sc, 2sc in next stitch, repeat from * to complete round (12 sts).
Rounds 4–5: Sc in each stitch.
Round 6: * Sc, sc dec, repeat from * to complete round (8 sts).
Round 7: Sc dec 4 times. Sl st to first stitch of round.
Fasten off, leaving a long tail to sew onto hat.

Tooth

Using Color B, ch4.
Row 1: Turn, sc3 (3 sts).
Rows 2–3: Turn, ch1, sc3.
Fasten off. Weave in ends.

Finishing

Using yarn needle, sew eyes onto front and spikes onto sides of hat. Using Color F and crochet hook, sl st mouth onto hat. It doesn't have to be perfect, it's just silly! Using yarn needle, sew tooth onto mouth. Sew buttons onto eyes to finish.

Ahoy Matey!
Pirate Hat

Arrrgh! Join the crew and crochet this fun hat for your kids and all their mateys!

Skill Level

Beginner

Finished Measurements

Head circumference: Small: 15–17.5"/38–44.5 cm, Medium: 17.5–19"/44.5–48 cm, Large: 19–22.5"/48–57 cm, X-Large: 23–24.5"/58.5–68 cm
Height: Small: 6–6.5"/15–16.5 cm, Medium: 6.5–7"/16.5–18 cm, Large: 7–7.5"/18–19 cm, X-Large: 7.5–8"/19–20.5 cm

Yarn

- Lion Brand Vanna's Choice, medium worsted weight #4 yarn (100% acrylic; 170 yd/3.5 oz, 155 m/100 g per skein)
    1 skein #860-180 Cranberry (Color A)
    1 skein #860-100 White (Color B)
    1 skein #860-153 Black (Color C)

Hook and Other Materials

- H-8 (5.0 mm) hook or size to obtain gauge
- 2 stitch markers

Gauge

15 sts and 8 rows in dc = 4"/10 cm square

Notes

1. The hat is worked from the top down.
2. The ch2 at the beginning of each round does not count as a stitch.
3. After completing the beanie, you will crochet the ties onto the last row. To finish, you will add the eye patch directly onto the last row of ties.
4. To change colors, push hook through the last stitch of the first color, pull yarn back through, yarn over with the NEXT color, and pull through. Color change is complete. Also see page 131 for a tutorial.
5. When you change colors, you will carry the old yarn instead of fastening it off. That will allow you to simply pick the yarn up later with no ends to weave in. For a tutorial, see page 132.
6. See page 126 for a tutorial on Single Crochet Decrease (sc dec).

Hat

SMALL

Using Color A, ch4.
Round 1: 8dc in fourth chain from hook, sl st to first stitch to join round (8 sts).
Round 2: Drop Color A, pick up Color B, ch2, 2dc in each stitch, sl st to first stitch to join round (16 sts).
Round 3: Drop Color B, pick up Color A, ch2, * dc, 2dc in next stitch, repeat from * to complete round, sl st to first stitch to join (24 sts).
Round 4: Drop Color A, pick up Color B, ch2, * dc2, 2dc in next stitch, repeat from * to complete round, sl st to first stitch to join (32 sts).
Round 5: Drop Color B, pick up Color A, ch2, * dc3, 2dc in next stitch, repeat from * to complete round, sl st to first stitch to join (40 sts).
Round 6: Drop Color A, pick up Color B, ch2, * dc4, 2dc in next stitch, repeat from * to complete round, sl st to first stitch to join (48 sts).
Round 7: Drop Color B, pick up Color A, ch2, dc in each stitch, sl st to first stitch to join.
Round 8: Drop Color A, pick up Color B, ch2, dc in each stitch, sl st to first stitch to join.
Rounds 9–10: Repeat Rounds 7 and 8.
Fasten off. Weave in ends.

MEDIUM

Using Color A, ch4.
Round 1: 10dc in fourth chain from hook, sl st to first stitch to join round (10 sts).
Round 2: Drop Color A, pick up Color B, ch2, 2dc in each stitch, sl st to first stitch to join (20 sts).
Round 3: Drop Color B, pick up Color A, ch2, * dc, 2dc in next stitch, repeat from * to complete round, sl st to first stitch to join (30 sts).
Round 4: Drop Color A, pick up Color B, ch2, * dc2, 2dc in next stitch, repeat from * to complete round, sl st to first stitch to join (40 sts).
Round 5: Drop Color B, pick up Color A, ch2, * dc3, 2dc in next stitch, repeat from * to complete round, sl st to first stitch to join (50 sts).
Round 6: Drop Color A, pick up Color B, ch2, * dc4, 2dc in next stitch, repeat from * to complete round, sl st to first stitch to join (60 sts).
Round 7: Drop Color B, pick up Color A, ch2, dc in each stitch, sl st to first stitch to join.
Round 8: Drop Color A, pick up Color B, ch2, dc in each stitch, sl st to first stitch to join.
Rounds 9–12: Repeat Rounds 7 and 8 twice.
Fasten off. Weave in ends.

LARGE

Using Color A, ch4.

Round 1: 12dc in fourth chain from hook, sl st to first stitch to join round (12 sts).

Round 2: Drop Color A, pick up Color B, ch2, 2dc in each stitch, sl st to first stitch to join (24 sts).

Round 3: Drop Color B, pick up Color A, ch2, * dc, 2dc in next stitch, repeat from * to complete round, sl st to first stitch to join (36 sts).

Round 4: Drop Color A, pick up Color B, ch2, * dc2, 2dc in next stitch, repeat from * to complete round, sl st to first stitch to join (48 sts).

Round 5: Drop Color B, pick up Color A, ch2, * dc3, 2dc in next stitch, repeat from * to complete round, sl st to first stitch to join (60 sts).

Round 6: Drop Color A, pick up Color B, ch2, * dc4, 2dc in next stitch, repeat from * to complete round, sl st to first stitch to join (72 sts).

Round 7: Drop Color B, pick up Color A, ch2, dc in each stitch, sl st to first stitch to join.

Round 8: Drop Color A, pick up Color B, ch2, dc in each stitch, sl st to first stitch to join.

Rounds 9–10: Repeat Rounds 7 and 8.

Round 11: Repeat Round 7.

Round 12: Drop Color A, pick up Color B, ch2, * dc5, dc dec, repeat from * to complete round, sl st to first stitch to join round (60 sts).

Rounds 13–14: Repeat Rounds 7 and 8.

Fasten off. Weave in ends.

X-LARGE

Using Color A, ch4.

Round 1: 12dc in fourth chain from hook, sl st to first stitch to join round (12 sts).

Round 2: Drop Color A, pick up Color B, ch2, 2dc in each stitch, sl st to first stitch to join round (24 sts).

Round 3: Drop Color B, pick up Color A, ch2, * dc, 2dc in next stitch, repeat from * to complete round, sl st to first stitch to join (36 sts).

Round 4: Drop Color A, pick up Color B, ch2, * dc2, 2dc in next stitch, repeat from * to complete round, sl st to first stitch to join (48 sts).

Round 5: Drop Color B, pick up Color A, ch2, * dc3, 2dc in next stitch, repeat from * to complete round, sl st to first stitch to join (60 sts).

Round 6: Drop Color A, pick up Color B, ch2, dc in each stitch, sl st to first stitch to join (60 sts).

Round 7: Drop Color B, pick up Color A, ch2, dc in each stitch, sl st to first stitch to join.

Rounds 8–13: Repeat Rounds 6 and 7 three times.

Round 14: Repeat Round 6

Fasten off. Weave in ends.

Ties

Fold hat in half with the seam in back and mark each side with a stitch marker. One side will be for ties and the other will assist with the eye patch placement.

After the ties are completed, knot loosely to finish.

SMALL

Row 1: Using Color A, ch 30, sc in one of the marked stitches and in each stitch around beanie, ch31 (109 sts).

Row 2: Turn, sc in second chain from hook and in each chain, sc48 around beanie, sc in each chain to end (108 sts).

Row 3: Turn, 2sc in first stitch, sc106, 2sc in last stitch (110 sts).

Row 4: Turn, 2sc in first stitch, sc108, 2sc in last stitch (112 sts).

Row 5: Turn, 2sc in first stitch, sc110, 2sc in last stitch (114 sts).

Fasten off. Weave in ends.

MEDIUM

Row 1: Using Color A, ch50, sc in one of the marked stitches and in each stitch around beanie, ch51 (161 sts).

Row 2: Turn, sc in second chain from hook and in each chain, sc60 around beanie, sc in each chain to end (160 sts).

Row 3: Turn, 2sc in first stitch, sc158, 2sc in last stitch (162 sts).

Row 4: Turn, 2sc in first stitch, sc160, 2sc in last stitch (164 sts).

Row 5: Turn, 2sc in first stitch, sc162, 2sc in last stitch (166 sts).

Fasten off. Weave in ends.

LARGE & X-LARGE

Row 1: Using Color A, ch50, sc in one of the marked stitches and in each stitch around beanie, ch51 (161 sts).
Row 2: Turn, sc in second chain from hook and in each chain, sc60 around beanie, sc in each chain to end (160 sts).
Row 3: Turn, 2sc in first stitch, sc158, 2sc in last stitch (162 sts).
Row 4: Turn, 2sc in first stitch, sc160, 2sc in last stitch (164 sts).
Row 5: Turn, 2sc in first stitch, sc162, 2sc in last stitch (166 sts).
Row 6: Turn, 2sc in first stitch, sc164, 2sc in last stitch (168 sts).
Fasten off. Weave in ends.

Eye Patch

SMALL & MEDIUM

Counting to the front, join Color C 18 stitches from other stitch marker, ch1.
Row 1: Sc10 across stitches of last row of ties (10 sts).
Rows 2–7: Turn, ch1, sc in each stitch.
Row 8: Turn, sc dec, sc6, sc dec (8 sts).
Row 9: Turn, sc dec, sc4, sc dec (6 sts).
Row 10: Turn, sc dec, sc2, sc dec (4 sts).
Row 11: Turn, sc dec twice (2 sts).
Fasten off. Weave in ends.

LARGE & X-LARGE

Counting to the front, join Color C 20 stitches from other stitch marker, ch1.
Row 1: Sc11 across stitches of last row (11 sts).
Rows 2–7: Turn, ch1, sc in each stitch.
Row 8: Turn, sc dec, sc7, sc dec (9 sts).
Row 9: Turn, sc dec, sc5, sc dec (7 sts).
Row 10: Turn, sc dec, sc3, sc dec (5 sts).
Row 11: Turn, sc dec, sc, sc dec (3 sts).
Fasten off. Weave in ends.

Bubblegum Machine Beanie

This hat is as fun as the machine it represents! It is a great scrap-buster project.

Skill Level

Intermediate

Finished Measurements

Head circumference: Small: 15–17.5"/38–44 cm, Medium: 17.5–19"/44.5–48 cm, Large: 19–22.5"/48–57 cm
Height: Small: 6–6.5"/15–16.5 cm, Medium: 6.5–7"/ 16.5–18 cm, Large: 7–7.5"/18–19 cm

Yarn

- Lion Brand Vanna's Choice, medium weight #4 yarn (100% acrylic; 170 yd/6.5 oz, 155 m/ 100 g per skein)
    1 skein #860-110 Navy (Color A)
    1 skein #860-100 White (Color B)
    1 skein #860-113 Scarlet (Color C)
    1 skein #860-102 Aqua (Color D)
    1 skein #840-157 Duckie (Color E)
    1 skein #840-169 Sweet Pea (Color F)
    1 skein #840-139 Berrylicious (Color G)
    1 skein #860-149 Silver Gray (Color H)
    1 skein #860-153 Black (Color I)

Hook and Other Materials

- H-8 (5.0 mm) hook or size to obtain gauge
- Yarn needle
- Stitch markers (optional)

Gauge

12 sts and 8 rows in dc = 4"/10 cm square

Notes

1. The hat is worked from the top down in the round. In the first part of the hat, the rounds are continuous. If you like, you can mark the beginning of each round with a stitch marker for reference.
2. The bubblegum drops, coin slot, and ties are made separately and then attached.
3. The bubblegum drop colors can be made with any scrap yarn you might have around, and do not have to be a specific color.
4. See page 129 for a tutorial on Front Post Double Crochet (fpdc), page 130 for Back Post Double Crochet (bpdc), and page 126 for Single Crochet Decrease (sc dec).

Hat

SMALL

Using Color C, ch2.
Round 1: 8sc in second chain from hook (8 sts).
Round 2: Working continuously in the round, 2sc in each stitch (16 sts).
Round 3: * Sc, 2sc in next stitch, repeat from * to complete round (24 sts).
Round 4: * Sc2, 2sc in next stitch, repeat from * to complete round (32 sts).
Round 5: * Sc3, 2sc in next stitch, repeat from * to complete round (40 sts).
Round 6: * Sc4, 2sc in next stitch, repeat from * to complete round (48 sts).
Rounds 7–8: Sc in each stitch.
Round 9: Join Color B, fasten off Color C, ch2, dc in each stitch, sl st to first stitch to join.
Rounds 10–14: Ch2, dc in each stitch, sl st to first stitch to join.
Round 15: Join Color C, fasten off Color B, ch2, dc in each stitch, sl st to first stitch to join.
Rounds 16–18: Ch2, * fpdc2, bpdc2, repeat from * to complete round, sl st to first stitch to join.
Fasten off. Weave in ends.

The ties are braided right onto the hat.

MEDIUM

Using Color C, ch2.
Round 1: 8sc in second chain from hook (8 sts).
Round 2: Working continuously in the round, 2sc in each stitch (16 sts).
Round 3: * Sc, 2sc in next stitch, repeat from * to complete round (24 sts).
Round 4: * Sc2, 2sc in next stitch, repeat from * to complete round (32 sts).
Round 5: * Sc3, 2sc in next stitch, repeat from * to complete round (40 sts).
Round 6: * Sc4, 2sc in next stitch, repeat from * to complete round (48 sts).
Round 7: * Sc5, 2sc in next stitch, repeat from * to complete round (54 sts).
Rounds 8–9: Sc in each stitch.
Round 10: Join Color B, fasten off Color C, ch2, dc in each stitch, sl st to first stitch to join.
Rounds 11–16: Ch2, dc in each stitch, sl st to first stitch to join.

Round 17: Join Color C, fasten off Color B, ch2, dc in each stitch, sl st to first stitch to join.
Rounds 18–20: Ch2, * fpdc2, bpdc2, repeat from * to complete round, sl st to first stitch to join.
Fasten off. Weave in ends.

LARGE

Using Color A, ch2.
Round 1: 8sc in second chain from hook (8 sts).
Round 2: Working continuously in the round, 2sc in each stitch (16 sts).
Round 3: * Sc, 2sc in next stitch, repeat from * to complete round (24 sts).
Round 4: * Sc2, 2sc in next stitch, repeat from * to complete round (32 sts).
Round 5: * Sc3, 2sc in next stitch, repeat from * to complete round (40 sts).
Round 6: * Sc4, 2sc in next stitch, repeat from * to complete round (48 sts).
Round 7: * Sc5, 2sc in next stitch, repeat from * to complete round (56 sts).

Round 8: * Sc6, 2sc in next stitch, repeat from * to complete round (64 sts).
Rounds 9–10: Sc in each stitch.
Round 11: Join Color B, fasten off Color C, ch2, dc in each stitch, sl st to first stitch to join.
Rounds 12–17: Ch2, dc in each stitch, sl st to first stitch to join.
Round 18: Join Color C, fasten off Color B, ch2, dc in each stitch, sl st to first stitch to join.
Rounds 19–22: Ch2, * fpdc2, bpdc2, repeat from * to complete round, sl st to first stitch to join.
Fasten off. Weave in ends.

Ties (make 2)

Place 2 stitch markers on opposite sides of the bottom round of the hat, counting to make sure markers are placed evenly. For each tie: Cut 6 lengths of yarn 3'/1 m long. Align the ends, then, holding them together, fold them in half. With a crochet hook, pull the center fold through the marked stitch. Take hold of the cut ends and thread them through the fold. Pull tight on the ends. Working with 3 groups of 4 strands each, braid the yarn, knot the ends, and trim to finish.

Bubblegum Drops

Using Colors A, C, D, E, F, and G, make 4 to 6 in each color. Ch2.
Round 1: 6sc in the first chain, sl st to join round (6 sts). Fasten off, leaving a long tail to sew onto hat.

Coin Slot

Using Color H, ch6.
Row 1: Sc in second chain from hook and in each chain across (5 sts).
Rows 2–6: Turn, ch1, sc in each stitch.
Row 7: Turn, sc dec, sc in next stitch, sc dec (3 sts).
Fasten off, leaving a long tail to sew onto hat.

Finishing

Using yarn needle, sew coin slot onto center front of hat. With yarn needle, sew gumballs in a random pattern onto white section of hat. Weave in ends.

Using Color I, loosely sl st across Row 5 of coin slot to create the slot. Fasten off. Weave in ends.

Downtown Girl Slouchy

Slouchy beanies are so hip for kids, teens, AND mom! You will be the coolest mom in town with this textured topper!

Skill Level

Intermediate

Finished Measurements

Head circumference: Small: 15–17.5"/38–44.5 cm, Medium: 17.5–19"/44.5–48 cm, Large: 19–22.5"/48–57 cm

Yarn

- Yarn Bee Enchantress, medium worsted weight #4 yarn (95% acrylic/5% payette; 160 yd/3.5 oz, 146 m/100 g per skein)
    - 2 skeins #601 Peony (Color A)
    - 2 skein #901 Gray Mist (Color B)

Hook and Other Materials

- H-8 (5.0 mm) hook or size to obtain gauge
- Sewing needle and thread

Gauge

16 sts and 4 rows in dc = 4"/10 cm square

Notes

1. The hat is worked as a panel and sewn together, then the brim is added.
2. The ch3 at the beginning of each row counts as the first dc.
3. See page 131 for a tutorial on Treble Crochet (tr), page 124 for crocheting into the Back Loop Only (blo), and page 97 for Back Post Single Crochet (bpsc).

Hat

SMALL

Using Color A, ch23.
Row 1: Turn, sc in each chain (23 sts).
Row 2: Turn, ch 3, skip next 3 stitches, tr in next stitch, ch1, working in front of tr just made, tr in second skipped stitch, * skip next 2 stitches, tr in next stitch, ch1, working in front of tr just made, tr in first skipped stitch, repeat from * to last stitch, dc in last stitch to complete row (23 sts).
Row 3: Turn, ch 3, dc in second stitch from hook and each stitch across (23 sts).
Row 4: Repeat Row 2.
Rows 5–22: Repeat Rows 3–4 nine times.
Rows 23–28: Ch1, sl st in blo of each stitch.
Fasten off, leaving a long tail to sew ends of panel together. Using yarn needle, sew the first and last row together. Fasten off. Weave in ends.

MEDIUM

Using Color A, ch26.
Row 1: Turn, sc in each chain (26 sts).

Row 2: Turn, ch 3, skip next 3 stitches, tr in next stitch, ch1, working in front of tr just made, tr in second skipped stitch, * skip next 2 stitches, tr in next stitch, ch1, working in front of tr just made, tr in first skipped stitch, repeat from * to last stitch, dc in last stitch to complete row (26 sts).
Row 3: Turn, ch 3, dc in second stitch from hook and each stitch across (26 sts).
Row 4: Repeat Row 2.
Rows 5–28: Repeat Rows 3–4 twelve times.
Rows 29–34: Ch1, sl st in blo of each stitch.
Fasten off, leaving a long tail to sew ends of panel together. Using yarn needle, sew the first and last row together. Fasten off. Weave in ends.

LARGE

Using Color B, ch29.
Row 1: Turn, sc in each chain (29 sts).
Row 2: Turn, ch 3, skip next 3 stitches, tr in next stitch, ch1, working in front of tr just made, tr in second skipped stitch, * skip next 2 stitches, tr in next stitch, ch1, working in front of tr just made, tr in first skipped stitch, repeat from * to last stitch, dc in last stitch to complete row (29 sts).
Row 3: Turn, ch 3, dc in second stitch from hook and each stitch across (29 sts).
Row 4: Repeat Row 2.
Rows 5–32: Repeat Rows 3–4 fourteen times.
Rows 33–38: Ch1, sl st in blo of each stitch.
Fasten off, leaving a long tail to sew ends of panel together. Using yarn needle, sew the first and last row together. Fasten off. Weave in ends.

Brim

Row 1: Working along the ends of rows on bottom edge, 2sc in each space, sl st to first stitch to join (48, 60, 66 sts).
Row 2: Ch1, bpsc in each stitch, sl st to first stitch to join.
Row 3: Ch1, sc in each stitch, sl st to first stitch to join.
Rows 4–5: Repeat Rows 2–3.
Fasten off. Weave in ends.

Finishing

Using yarn needle, weave a length of yarn in and out of stitches along top edge. Pull tight. Fasten off. Weave in ends.

The brim is worked onto the panel using the ends of the rows as stitches.

Rosey
Newsboy

Have a fun day in the sun with this newsboy-style hat! Change the colors and leave off the flower to make it for your favorite guys!

Skill Level

Intermediate

Finished Measurements

Head circumference: X-Small: 12–14.5"/30.5–37 cm, Small: 15–17.5"/38–44.5 cm, Medium: 17.5–19"/44.5–48 cm, Large: 19–22.5"/48–57 cm, X-Large: 23–24.5"/58.5–62 cm
Height: X-Small: 4.5–6"/11.5–15 cm, Small: 6–6.5"/15–16.5 cm, Medium: 6.5–7"/16.5–18 cm, Large: 7–7.5"/18–19 cm, X-Large: 7.5–8"/19–20.5 cm

Yarn

- Red Heart Super Saver, medium worsted weight #4 yarn (100% acrylic; 364 yd/7 oz, 333 m/198 g per skein) 1 skein #374 Country Rose (Color A)
- Caron One Pound, medium worsted weight #4 yarn (100% acrylic; 826 yd/16 oz, 755 m/454 g per skein) 1 skein #0514 Off White (Color B)

Hook and Other Materials

- H-8 (5.0 mm) hook or size to obtain gauge
- J-10 (6.0 mm) hook or size to obtain gauge (for X-Large size only)
- Yarn needle

Gauge

Using H-8 (5.0 mm) hook and Color A, 12 sts and 8 rows in dc = 4"/10 cm square
Using J-10 (6.0 mm) hook and Color A, 10 sts and 7 rows in dc = 4"/10 cm square

Notes

1. The hat is worked from the top down in rounds.
2. The visor will be added to the last row and the flower will be made separately and then sewn on with the yarn needle.
3. The ch2 at the beginning of each round does not count as a stitch.
4. To change colors, push the hook through the last stitch of the first color, pull the yarn back through, yarn over with the NEXT color, and pull through. Color change is complete. Also see page 131 for a tutorial.
5. When you change colors, you will carry the old yarn instead of fastening it off. That will allow you to simply pick the yarn up later with no ends to weave in. For a tutorial, see page 132.
6. See page 128 for a tutorial on Double Crochet Decrease (dc dec) and page 126 for Single Crochet Decrease (sc dec).

Special Technique
Front Post Treble (fptr)

1 Yarn over 2 times, insert hook around post of stitch from front to back to front, yarn over, and pull up a loop: 4 loops on hook.

2 Yarn over; pull through first 2 loops on hook: 3 loops on hook.

(continued)

3 Yarn over; pull through 2 loops on hook: 2 loops on hook.

4 Yarn over; pull through last 2 loops on hook. Front post treble is complete.

Hat

X-SMALL

Using H-8 (5.0 mm) hook and Color A, ch4.
Round 1: 9dc in fourth chain from hook, sl st to first stitch to join round (9 sts).
Round 2: Ch2, 2dc in each stitch, sl st to first stitch to join (18 sts).
Round 3: Ch2, * dc, 2dc in next stitch, repeat from * to complete round, sl st to first stitch to join (27 sts).
Round 4: Ch2, * dc2, 2dc in next stitch, repeat from * to complete round, sl st to first stitch to join (36 sts).
Round 5: Drop Color A, pick up Color B, ch2, * dc, fptr (see Special Technique), repeat from * to complete round, sl st to first stitch to join.
Round 6: Drop Color B, pick up Color A, ch2, * fptr, dc, repeat from * to complete round, sl st to first stitch to join.
Round 7: Repeat Round 5.

Round 8: Fasten off Color B, pick up Color A, ch2, * fptr, dc, repeat from * to complete round, sl st to first stitch to join.
Rounds 9–10: Ch2, dc in each stitch, sl st to first stitch to join.
Fasten off. Weave in ends.

SMALL

Using H-8 (5.0 mm) hook and color A, ch4.
Round 1: 8dc in fourth chain from hook, sl st to first stitch to join round (8 sts).
Round 2: Ch2, 2dc in each stitch, sl st to first stitch to join (16 sts).
Round 3: Ch2, * dc, 2dc in next stitch, repeat from * to complete round, sl st to first stitch to join (24 sts).
Round 4: Ch2, * dc2, 2dc in next stitch, repeat from * to complete round, sl st to first stitch to join (32 sts).
Round 5: Ch2, * dc3, 2dc in next stitch, repeat from * to complete round, sl st to first stitch to join (40 sts).
Round 6: Drop Color A, pick up Color B, ch2, * dc, fptr (see Special Technique), repeat from * to complete round, sl st to first stitch to join.
Round 7: Drop Color B, pick up Color A, ch2, * fptr, dc, repeat from * to complete round, sl st to first stitch to join.
Round 8: Repeat Round 6.
Round 9: Fasten off Color B, pick up Color A, ch2, * fptr, dc, repeat from * to complete round, sl st to first stitch to join.
Rounds 10–11: Ch2, dc in each stitch, sl st to first stitch to join.
Fasten off. Weave in ends.

MEDIUM

Using H-8 (5.0 mm) hook and color A, ch4.
Round 1: 10dc in fourth chain from hook, sl st to first stitch to join round (10 sts).
Round 2: Ch2, 2dc in each stitch, sl st to first stitch to join (20 sts).
Round 3: Ch2, * dc, 2dc in next stitch, repeat from * to complete round, sl st to first stitch to join (30 sts).
Round 4: Ch2, * dc2, 2dc in next stitch, repeat from * to complete round, sl st to first stitch to join (40 sts).
Round 5: Ch2, * dc3, 2dc in next stitch, repeat from * to complete round, sl st to first stitch to join (50 sts).
Round 6: Drop Color A, pick up Color B, ch2, * dc, fptr (see Special Technique), repeat from * to complete round, sl st to first stitch to join.
Round 7: Drop Color B, pick up Color A, ch2, * fptr, dc, repeat from * to complete round, sl st to first stitch to join.
Rounds 8–9: Repeat Rounds 6–7.
Round 10: Repeat Round 6.
Round 11: Fasten off Color B, pick up Color A, ch2, * fptr, dc, repeat from * to complete round, sl st to first stitch to join.
Rounds 12–13: Ch2, dc in each stitch, sl st to first stitch to join.
Fasten off. Weave in ends.

LARGE

Using H-5.0 mm hook and color A, ch4.
Round 1: 10dc in fourth chain from hook, sl st to first stitch to join round (10 sts).
Round 2: Ch2, 2dc in each stitch, sl st to first stitch to join (20 sts).
Round 3: Ch2, * dc, 2dc in next stitch, repeat from * to complete round, sl st to first stitch to join (30 sts).
Round 4: Ch2, * dc2, 2dc in next stitch, repeat from * to complete round, sl st to first stitch to join (40 sts).
Round 5: Ch2, * dc3, 2dc in next stitch, repeat from * to complete round, sl st to first stitch to join (50 sts).
Round 6: Ch2, * dc4, 2dc in next stitch, repeat from * to complete round, sl st to first stitch to join (60 sts).
Round 7: Drop Color A, pick up Color B, ch2, * dc, fptr (see Special Technique), repeat from * to complete round, sl st to first stitch to join.
Round 8: Drop Color B, pick up Color A, ch2, * fptr, dc, repeat from * to complete round, sl st to first stitch to join.
Rounds 9–12: Repeat Rounds 7 and 8 twice.
Round 13: Repeat Round 7.
Round 14: Fasten off Color B, pick up Color A, ch2, * fptr, dc, repeat from * to complete round, sl st to first stitch to join.
Round 15: Ch2, * dc8, dc dec, repeat from * to complete round (54 sts).
Round 16: Ch2, dc in each stitch, sl st to first stitch to join.
Fasten off. Weave in ends.

X-LARGE

Using J-10 (6.0 mm) hook, follow instructions for Large size.

Visor

Fold hat in half and mark opposite sides on the last round with stitch markers.

X-SMALL

Using H-8 (5.0 mm) hook and Color A, join yarn at a marker.
Row 1: Ch1, sc18 in stitches across last row of hat (18 sts).
Rows 2–3: Turn, ch1, sc to end of row.
Row 4: Turn, sc dec, sc14, sc dec (16 sts).
Row 5: Turn, sc dec, sc12, sc dec (14 sts).
Row 6: Turn, sc dec, sc10, sc dec (12 sts).
Fasten off. Weave in ends.

SMALL

Using H-8 (5.0 mm) hook and Color A, join yarn at a marker.
Row 1: Ch1, sc20 in stitches across last row of hat (20 sts).
Rows 2–4: Turn, ch1, sc to end of row.
Row 5: Turn, sc dec, sc16, sc dec (18 sts).
Row 6: Turn, sc dec, sc14, sc dec (16 sts).
Row 7: Turn, sc dec, sc12, sc dec (14 sts).
Fasten off. Weave in ends.

MEDIUM, LARGE & X-LARGE

Using H-8 (5.0 mm) hook (for X-large, use J-10 [6.0 mm] hook) and color A, join yarn at a marker.
Row 1: Ch1, sc25 in stitches across last row of hat (25 sts).
Rows 2–5: Turn, ch1, sc to end of row.
Row 6: Turn, sc dec, sc21, sc dec (23 sts).
Row 7: Turn, sc dec, sc19, sc dec (21 sts).
Row 8: Turn, sc dec, sc17, sc dec (19 sts).
Fasten off. Weave in ends.

LAST ROUND (ALL SIZES)

Join yarn in any stitch of last row. Sc in each stitch around hat, including visor, to complete the round.
Fasten off. Weave in ends.

Flower

Using H-8 (5.0 mm) hook and Color B, ch25.
Row 1: (Dc, ch1, dc, ch1) in fourth chain from hook, * (dc, ch1, dc, ch1) in next chain, repeat from * to last chain. In last chain, (dc, ch1, dc, ch1) two times. Working on opposite side of chain, repeat from * to end, sl st to first stitch to join round.
Fasten off, leaving a long tail to sew together.

 Roll the flower and, using yarn needle, sew together at base and then sew onto hat.

Giggles & Curls Hat

Laughter and merriment are a guarantee with this hat! Make in a variety of colors and add pom-poms for a boy instead of curls!

Skill Level

Intermediate

Finished Measurements

Head circumference: X-Small: 12–14.5"/30.5–37 cm, Small: 15–17.5"/38–44.5 cm, Medium: 17.5–19"/44.5–48 cm, Large: 19–22.5/48–57 cm"
Height: X-Small: 4.5–6"/11.5–15 cm, Small: 6–6.5"/ 15–16.5 cm, Medium: 6.5–7"/16.5–18 cm, Large: 7–7.5"/ 18–19 cm

Yarn

• Lily Sugar'n Cream, medium worsted weight #4 yarn (100% cotton; 200 yd/4 oz, 183 m/113 g per skein)
    1 skein #1712 Hot Green (Color A)
    1 skein #1742 Hot Blue (Color B)

Hook and Other Materials

• G-7 (4.75 mm) hook or size to obtain gauge
• Yarn needle

Gauge

14 sts and 12 rows in sc = 4"/10 cm square

Notes

1. The hat is worked in two parts. The top panel is created first, then sewn together. The brim is crocheted directly onto the hat.
2. When you change colors, you will carry the old yarn, instead of fastening it off. That will allow you to simply pick the yarn up later with no ends to weave in. For a tutorial, see page 132.
3. See page 126 for Single Crochet Decrease (sc dec), and page 124 for crocheting into the Back Loop Only (blo).

Special Technique
Front Post Single Crochet (fpsc)

1 Insert the hook around the post from the front to the back to the front of the stitch (see Anatomy of a Stitch on page 124 for where the post is located).

2 Yarn over and pull up a loop: 2 loops on hook.

3 Yarn over and draw the yarn through the 2 loops on hook to complete the stitch.

Hat

X-SMALL

Using Color A, ch13.
Row 1: Turn, sc in second chain from hook and in each ch across (12 sts).
Row 2: Drop Color A, join Color B, turn, ch1, fpsc in each stitch.
Row 3: Turn, ch1, sc in each stitch.
Row 4: Drop Color B, pick up Color A, turn, ch1, fpsc in each stitch.
Row 5: Turn, ch1, sc in each stitch.
Row 6: Drop Color A, join Color B, turn, ch1, fpsc in each stitch.
Row 7: Turn, ch1, sc in each stitch.
Rows 8–39: Repeat Rows 4–7 nine times.
Fasten off, leaving a long tail to sew together.
   Fold piece in half. Using the yarn needle, sew the top and side edges together.
   Fasten off. Weave in ends.

SMALL

Using Color A, ch15.
Row 1: Turn, sc in second chain from hook and in each ch across (14 sts).
Row 2: Drop Color A, join Color B, turn, ch1, fpsc in each stitch.

Row 3: Turn, ch1, sc in each stitch.
Row 4: Drop Color B, pick up Color A, turn, ch1, fpsc in each stitch.
Row 5: Turn, ch1, sc in each stitch.
Row 6: Drop Color A, pick up Color B, turn, ch1, fpsc in each stitch.
Row 7: Turn, ch1, sc in each stitch.
Rows 8–47: Repeat Rows 4–7 ten times.
Fasten off, leaving a long tail to sew together.
   Fold piece in half. Using the yarn needle, sew the top and side edges together.
   Fasten off. Weave in ends.

MEDIUM

Using Color A, ch18.
Row 1: Turn, sc in second chain from hook and in each ch across (17 sts).
Row 2: Drop Color A, join Color B, turn, ch1, fpsc in each stitch.
Row 3: Turn, ch1, sc in each stitch.
Row 4: Drop Color B, pick up Color A, turn, ch1, fpsc in each stitch.
Row 5: Turn, ch1, sc in each stitch.
Row 6: Drop Color A, pick up Color B, turn, ch1, fpsc in each stitch.
Row 7: Turn, ch1, sc in each stitch.
Rows 8–59: Repeat Rows 4–7 thirteen times.
Fasten off, leaving a long tail to sew together.

Fold piece in half. Using the yarn needle, sew the top and side edges together.

Fasten off. Weave in ends.

LARGE

Using Color A, ch21.

Row 1: Turn, sc in second chain from hook and in each ch across (20 sts).

Row 2: Drop Color A, join Color B, turn, ch1, fpsc in each stitch.

Row 3: Turn, ch1, sc in each stitch.

Row 4: Drop Color B, pick up Color A, turn, ch1, fpsc in each stitch.

Row 5: Turn, ch1, sc in each stitch.

Row 6: Drop Color A, pick up Color B, turn, ch1, fpsc in each stitch.

Row 7: Turn, ch1, sc in each stitch.

Rows 8–75: Repeat Rows 4–7 seventeen times.

Fasten off, leaving a long tail to sew together.

Fold piece in half. Using the yarn needle, sew the top and side edges together.

Fasten off. Weave in ends.

Brim

Using Color B, join yarn at seam of hat.

X-SMALL

Round 1: Ch1, using ends of rows as stitches, loosely sl st in each stitch around, sl st to first stitch to join (40 sts).

Round 2: Ch1, sc in blo of each stitch, sl st to first stitch to join.

Rounds 3–5: Ch1, sc in each stitch, sl st to first stitch to join.

Fasten off, weave in ends.

SMALL

Round 1: Ch1, using ends of rows as stitches, loosely sl st in each stitch around, sl st to ch1 to first stitch to join (48 sts).

Round 2: Ch1, sc in blo of each stitch, sl st to first stitch to join.

Rounds 3–5: Ch1, sc in each stitch, sl st to first stitch to join.

Fasten off, weave in ends.

MEDIUM

Round 1: Ch1, using ends of rows as stitches, loosely sl st in each stitch around, sl st to ch1 to first stitch to join (60 sts).

Round 2: Ch1, sc in blo of each stitch, sl st to first stitch to join.

Rounds 3–5: Ch1, sc in each stitch, sl st to first stitch to join.

Fasten off, weave in ends.

LARGE

Round 1: Ch1, using ends of rows as stitches, loosely sl st in each stitch around, sl st to ch1 to first stitch to join (76 sts).

Round 2: Ch1, sc in blo of each stitch, sl st to first stitch to join.

Rounds 3–4: Ch1, sc in each stitch, sl st to first stitch to join.

Round 5: Ch1, sc6, * sc8, sc dec, repeat from * to complete round, sl st to first stitch to join (70 sts).

Round 6: Ch1, * sc12, sc dec, repeat from * to complete round, sl st to first stitch to join (65 sts).

Rounds 7–8: Ch1, sc in each stitch, sl st to first stitch to join.

Fasten off, weave in ends.

Curls

SHORT CURLS (MAKE 4)

Using Color B, ch16.

Row 1: Turn, 2sc in second chain from hook and in each chain (30 sts).

Fasten off, leaving a long tail to sew onto hat.

LONG CURL (MAKE 2)

Using Color B, ch26.

Row 1: Turn, 2sc in second chain from hook and in each chain (50 sts).

Fasten off, leaving a long tail to sew onto hat.

Finishing

Using yarn needle, attach 2 short curls and 1 long curl to each top corner of hat. Weave in ends.

Baby Doll Hat

Th

his hat is perfect for dress up, costumes, or gifts. It has also been a big hit as a chemo cap for children.

Skill Level
Advanced

Finished Measurements
Head circumference: X-Small: 12–14.5"/30.5–37 cm, Small: 15–17.5"/38–44.5 cm, Medium: 17.5–19"/44.5–48 cm, Large: 19–22.5"/48–57 cm

Yarn
- Red Heart Super Saver, medium worsted weight #4 yarn (100% acrylic; 364 yd/7 oz, 333 m/199 oz per skein)
    - 1 skein #0718 Shocking Pink (Color A)
    - 1 skein #0512 Turqua (Color B)
    - 1 skein #0776 Dark Orchid (Color C)

Hook and Other Materials
- G-6 (4.0 mm) hook or size needed to obtain gauge
- Yarn needle

Gauge
12 sts and 11 rows in dc= 4"/10 cm square

Notes
1. The hat is worked from the top down in rounds. After finishing the beanie, you will then work in rows back and forth to create the lower portion of the hat.
2. The ch2 at the beginning of each round does not count as a stitch. However, the ch3 at the beginning of the rows does.
3. See page 129 for a tutorial on Front Post Double Crochet, page 130 for Back Post Double Crochet, and page 124 for crocheting into the Back Loop Only (blo).

Hat

X-SMALL
Using Color A, ch4.
Round 1: 10dc in fourth chain from hook, sl st to first stitch to join round (10 sts).
Round 2: Ch2, 2fpdc in each stitch, sl st to first stitch to join (20 sts).
Round 3: Ch2, * fpdc, (dc, fpdc) in next stitch, repeat from * to complete round, sl st to first stitch to join (30 sts).
Round 4: Ch2, * (dc, fpdc) in next stitch, dc, fpdc, repeat from * to complete round, sl st to first stitch to join (40 sts).
Rounds 5–12: Ch2, * dc, fpdc, repeat from * to complete round, sl st to first stitch to join.
Row 13: Turn, ch3, * bpdc, dc, repeat from * 13 times (27 sts).
Row 14: Turn, ch3, * fpdc, dc, repeat from * to end of row.
Row 15: Turn, ch3, * bpdc, dc, repeat from * to end of row.
Rows 16–23: Repeat Rows 14–15 four times.
Row 24: Repeat Row 14.
Fasten off. Weave in ends.

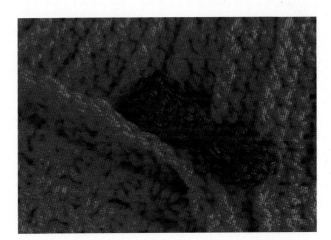

The small bow adds a fun finishing touch to this darling hat. You could also substitute a flower pattern from another hat!

SMALL

Using Color A, ch4.

Round 1: 8dc in fourth chain from hook, sl st to first stitch to join round (8 sts).

Round 2: Ch2, 2fpdc in each stitch, sl st to first stitch to join (16 sts).

Round 3: Ch2, * fpdc, (dc, fpdc) in next stitch, repeat from * to complete round, sl st to first stitch to join (24 sts).

Round 4: Ch2, * (dc, fpdc) in next stitch, dc, fpdc, repeat from * to complete round, sl st to first stitch to join (32 sts).

Round 5: Ch2, * 2dc in next stitch, fpdc, dc, fpdc, repeat from * to complete round, sl st to first stitch to join (40 sts).

Round 6: Ch2, dc2, fpdc, 2dc in next stitch, fpdc, repeat from * to complete round, sl st to first stitch to join (48 sts).

Rounds 7–15: Ch2, * dc2, fpdc in next stitch, dc2, fpdc, repeat from * to complete round, sl st to first stitch to join (48 sts).

Row 16: Turn, ch3, * bpdc, dc2, bpdc, dc2, repeat from * 5 more times (37 sts).

Row 17: Turn, ch3, dc, fpdc, dc2, fpdc, *dc2, fpdc, dc2, fpdc, repeat from * to last st, dc in last st (37 sts).

Row 18: Turn, ch3, * bpdc, dc2, bpdc, dc2, repeat from * to complete row.

Rows 19–26: Repeat Rows 21–22 four times.

Fasten off. Weave in ends.

MEDIUM

Using Color B, ch4.

Round 1: 11dc in fourth chain from hook, sl st to first stitch to join round (11 sts).

Round 2: Ch2, 2fpdc in each stitch, sl st to first stitch to join (22 sts).

Round 3: Ch2, * fpdc, (dc, fpdc) in next stitch, repeat from * to complete round, sl st to first stitch to join (33 sts).

Round 4: Ch2, * (dc, fpdc) in next stitch, dc, fpdc, repeat from * to complete round, sl st to first stitch to join (44 sts).

Round 5: Ch2, * 2dc in next stitch, fpdc, dc, fpdc, repeat from * to complete round, sl st to first stitch to join (55 sts).

Rounds 6–17: Ch2, * dc2, fpdc, dc, fpdc, repeat from * to complete round, sl st to first stitch to join (55 sts).

Row 18: Turn, ch3, * bpdc, dc, bpdc, dc2, repeat from * 6 more times (36 sts).

Row 19: Turn, ch3, dc, fpdc, dc, fpdc, * dc2, fpdc, dc, fpdc, repeat from * to last stitch, dc in last stitch.

Row 20: Turn, ch3, * bpdc, dc, bpdc, dc2, repeat from * to complete row.

Rows 21–26: Repeat Rows 19–20 three times.

Row 27: Repeat Row 19.

Fasten off. Weave in ends.

LARGE

Using Color B, ch4.

Round 1: 10dc in fourth chain from hook, sl st to first stitch to join round (10 sts).

Round 2: Ch2, 2fpdc in each stitch, sl st to first stitch to join (20 sts).

Round 3: Ch2, * fpdc, (dc, fpdc) in next stitch, repeat from * to complete round, sl st to first stitch to join (30 sts).

Round 4: Ch2, * (dc, fpdc) in next stitch, dc, fpdc, repeat from * to complete round, sl st to first stitch to join (40 sts).

Round 5: Ch2, * 2dc in next stitch, fpdc, dc, fpdc, repeat from * to complete round, sl st to first stitch to join (50 sts).

Round 6: Ch2, * 2dc in next stitch, dc, fpdc, dc, fpdc, repeat from * to complete round, sl st to first stitch to join (60 sts).

Round 7: Ch2, * dc3, fpdc, 2dc in next stitch, fpdc, repeat from * to complete round, sl st to first stitch to join (70 sts).

Rounds 8–19: Ch2, * dc3, fpdc in next stitch, dc2, fpdc, repeat from * to complete round, sl st to first stitch to join (70 sts).

Row 20: Turn, ch3, * bpdc, dc2, bpdc, dc3, repeat from * 7 more times (57 sts).

Row 21: Turn, ch3, dc2, fpdc, dc2, fpdc, *dc3, fpdc, dc2, fpdc, repeat from * to last st, dc in last st (57 sts).

Row 22: Turn, ch3, * bpdc, dc2, bpdc, dc3, repeat from * to complete row.

Rows 23–30: Repeat Rows 21–22 four times.

Fasten off. Weave in ends.

Bow

Using Color C, ch22, sl st to first ch to join.

Row 1: Ch1, sc in each chain, sl st to first stitch to join (22 sts).

Row 2: Ch1, sc in blo of each stitch, sl st to first stitch to join (22 sts).

Row 3: Ch1, sc in each stitch, sl st to first stitch to join (22 sts).

Fasten off, leaving a long tail to tie center of ribbon.

Lay ring flat and wrap yarn tail tightly around center 6 to 7 times.

Fasten off. Weave in ends.

Zack the Zombie

Creep up on your friends and surprise them with this zombie hat! Zombies are often scary characters, but this hat brings a childlike twist to the undead—it's not only the silliest zombie hat ever, it's also a blast to wear!

Skill Level
Beginner

Finished Measurements
Head circumference: X-Small: 12–14.5"/30.5–37 cm, Small: 15–17.5"/38–44.5 cm, Medium: 17.5–19"/44.5–48 cm, Large: 19–22.5"/48–57 cm, X-Large: 23–24.5"/58.5–62 cm
Height: X-Small: 4.5–6"/11.5–15 cm, Small: 6–6.5"/15–16.5 cm, Medium: 6.5–7"/16.5–18 cm, Large: 7–7.5"/18–19 cm, X-Large: 7.5–8"/19–20.5 cm

Yarn
- Lion Brand Vanna's Choice, medium worsted weight #4 yarn (100% acrylic; 170 yd/3.5 oz, 155 m/100 g per skein)
  1 skein #860-XX (Color A)
  1 skein #860-100 White (Color B)
- Yarn Bee Haute Fur Yarn, super bulky weight #6 yarn (100% exoline; 77 yd/3.5 oz, 70 m/100 g per skein)
  1 skein #121780 Cypress (Color C)

Hook and Other Materials
- H-8 (5.0 mm) hook or size to obtain gauge
- Stitch markers (optional)
- Fiberfill
- 2 small black buttons
- Yarn needle
- Sewing needle and thread

Gauge
13 sts and 15 rows in sc = 4"/10 cm square

Notes
1. The hat is worked from the top down in continuous rounds. If you like, you can use a stitch marker to mark the first stitch of each round for reference.
2. The hat will be made first; the earflaps, eyes, ears, and teeth will be added separately.
3. The ears are begun in the round, then worked back and forth in rows
4. See page 124 for a tutorial on crocheting through the Back Loop Only (blo), and page 121 for Single Crochet Decrease (sc dec).

Hat

X-SMALL
Using Color A and C together, ch4, sl st to first chain to create a ring.
Round 1: Ch1, 8sc in ring (8 sts).
Round 2: Working continuously in the round, 2sc in each stitch (16 sts).
Round 3: * Sc, 2sc in next stitch, repeat from * to complete round (24 sts).
Round 4: * Sc2, 2sc in next stitch, repeat from * to complete round (32 sts).
Round 5: * Sc3, 2sc in next stitch, repeat from * to complete round (40 sts).
Round 6: Fasten off Color C. With Color A sc in blo of each stitch.
Rounds 7–18: Sc in each stitch.
Fasten off. Weave in ends.

SMALL
Using Color A and Color C together, ch4, sl st to first chain to create a ring.
Round 1: Ch1, 8sc in ring (8 sts).
Round 2: Working continuously in the round, 2sc in each stitch (16 sts).
Round 3: * Sc, 2sc in next stitch, repeat from * to complete round (24 sts).
Round 4: * Sc2, 2sc in next stitch, repeat from * to complete round (32 sts).
Round 5: * Sc3, 2sc in next stitch, repeat from * to complete round (40 sts).
Round 6: * Sc4, 2sc in next stitch, repeat from * to complete round (48 sts).
Round 7: Fasten off Color C. With Color A, sc in blo of each stitch.
Rounds 8–21: Sc in each stitch.
Fasten off. Weave in ends.

MEDIUM
Using Color A and Color C together, ch4, sl st to first chain to create a ring.
Round 1: Ch1, 8sc in ring (8 sts).
Round 2: Working continuously in the round, 2sc in each stitch (16 sts).
Round 3: * Sc, 2sc in next stitch, repeat from * to complete round (24 sts).
Round 4: * Sc2, 2sc in next stitch, repeat from * to complete round (32 sts).

Round 5: * Sc3, 2sc in next stitch, repeat from * to complete round (40 sts).
Round 6: * Sc4, 2sc in next stitch, repeat from * to complete round (48 sts).
Round 7: * Sc5, 2sc in next stitch, repeat from * to complete round (56 sts).
Round 8: Fasten off Color C. With Color A, sc in blo of each stitch.
Rounds 9–24: Sc in each stitch.
Fasten off. Weave in ends.

LARGE

Using Color A and Color C together, ch4, sl st to first chain to create a ring.
Round 1: Ch1, 8sc in ring (8 sts).
Round 2: Working continuously in the round, 2sc in each stitch (16 sts).
Round 3: * Sc, 2sc in next stitch, repeat from * to complete round (24 sts).
Round 4: * Sc2, 2sc in next stitch, repeat from * to complete round (32 sts).
Round 5: * Sc3, 2sc in next stitch, repeat from * to complete round (40 sts).
Round 6: * Sc4, 2sc in next stitch, repeat from * to complete round (48 sts).
Round 7: * Sc5, 2sc in next stitch, repeat from * to complete round (56 sts).

Round 8: * Sc6, 2sc in next stitch, repeat from * to complete round (64 sts).
Round 9: Fasten off Color C. With Color A, sc in blo of each stitch.
Rounds 10–29: Sc in each stitch.
Fasten off. Weave in ends.

X-LARGE

Using Color A and Color C together, ch4, sl st to first chain to create a ring.
Round 1: Ch1, 10sc in ring (10 sts).
Round 2: Working continuously in the round, 2sc in each stitch (20 sts).
Round 3: * Sc, 2sc in next stitch, repeat from * to complete round (30 sts).
Round 4: * Sc2, 2sc in next stitch, repeat from * to complete round (40 sts).
Round 5: * Sc3, 2sc in next stitch, repeat from * to complete round (50 sts).
Round 6: * Sc4, 2sc in next stitch, repeat from * to complete round (60 sts).
Round 7: * Sc5, 2sc in next stitch, repeat from * to complete round (70 sts).
Round 8: Fasten off Color C. With Color A, sc in blo of each stitch.
Rounds 9–25: Sc in each stitch.
Round 26: * Sc5, sc dec, repeat from * to complete round (60 sts).
Rounds 27–29: Sc in each stitch.
Fasten off. Weave in ends.

Earflaps

Fold hat in half and mark opposite sides on last round with stitch markers. Join Color A at a marker and follow pattern per size to complete earflaps.

X-SMALL, SMALL & MEDIUM

Using Color A, ch1.
Row 1: Sc9 (9 sts).
Rows 2–6: Turn, ch1, sc to end (9 sts).
Row 7: Turn, sc dec, sc5, sc dec (7 sts).
Row 8: Turn, sc dec, sc3, sc dec (5 sts).
Fasten off.
Repeat on other side of hat. Weave in ends.

LARGE & X-LARGE

Using Color A, ch1.
Row 1: Sc10 (10 sts).
Rows 2–8: Turn, ch1, sc to end (10 sts).
Row 9: Turn, sc dec, sc6, sc dec (8 sts).
Row 10: Turn, sc dec, sc4, sc dec (6 sts).
Fasten off.
   Repeat on other side of hat. Weave in ends.

Eyes & Teeth (make 1 of each size)

EYE 1

Using Color B, ch2.
Round 1: 4sc in second chain from hook (4 sts).
Round 2: Working continuously in the round, 2sc in each stitch (8 sts).
Round 3: * Sc, 2sc in next stitch, repeat from * to complete round (12 sts).
Round 4: * Sc2, 2sc in next stitch, repeat from * to complete round (16 sts).
Rounds 5–7: Sc in each stitch.
Round 8: * Sc2, sc dec, repeat from * to complete round, sl st to first stitch to join (12 sts).
Fasten off. Weave in ends.

EYE 2

Using Color A, ch2.
Round 1: 6sc in second chain from hook (6 sts).
Round 2: Working continuously in the round, 2sc in each stitch (12 sts).
Round 3: * Sc, 2sc in next stitch, repeat from * to complete round (18 sts).
Round 4: * Sc2, 2sc in next stitch, repeat from * to complete round (24 sts).
Rounds 5–6: Sc in each stitch.
Round 7: * Sc2, sc dec, repeat from * to complete round, sl st to first stitch to join (18 sts).

TOOTH 1

Locate middle stitch between earflaps. Join Color A, ch1.
Row 1: Sc3 (3 sts).
Row 2: Turn, ch1, sc3.
Row 3: Turn, sc3.
Fasten off. Weave in ends.

TOOTH 2

Join Color A 3 stitches to left of first tooth, ch1.
Row 1: Sc3 (3 sts).
Row 2: Turn, ch1, sc3.
Row 3: Turn, sc3.
Row 4: Turn, sc3.
Fasten off. Weave in ends.

Finishing

Using sewing needle and thread, sew buttons onto center of eyes. Stuff eyes with fiberfil and sew onto hat with yarn needle.

Using yarn needle, sew ears onto each side of hat. Weave in ends.

Ears (make 2)

Using Color A, ch2.
Round 1: 4sc in second chain from hook (4 sts).
Round 2: Working continuously in the round, 2sc in each stitch (8 sts).
Round 3: * Sc, 2sc in next stitch, repeat from * to complete round (12 sts).
Row 4: Sc3 (3 sts).
Rows 5–6: Turn, ch1, sc3 (3 sts).
Row 7: Turn, sc dec, using the middle stitch again, sc dec (2 sts).
Round 8: Sc around the ear, working a sl st in the corners between the two parts of the ear. Sl st to first stitch to join. Fasten off. Weave in ends.

Twisted Stitches Beanie

Bet you didn't think you could make cables with a crochet hook! The front post treble crochet stitch is what gives this fun hat its twisting stitches. It's perfect for boys, girls, men, and women!

Skill Level

Intermediate

Finished Measurements

Head circumference: Small: 15–17.5"/38–44.5 cm, Medium: 17.5–19"/44.5–48 cm, Large: 19–22.5"/48–57 cm
Height: Small: 6–6.5"/15–16.5 cm, Medium: 6.5–7"/16.5–18 cm, Large: 7–7.5"/18–19 cm

Yarn

- Lion Brand Wool-Ease Chunky, super bulky weight #6 yarn (80% acrylic/20% wool; 153 yd/5 oz, 140 m/142 g per skein)
    1 skein #127 Walnut (Color A)
    1 skein #173 Willow (Color B)

Hook and Other Materials

- H-8 (5.0 mm) hook or size to obtain gauge (for Small size only)
- K-10^1/$_2$ (6.5 mm) hook or size to obtain gauge

Gauge

Using H-8 (5.0 mm) hook: 14 sts and 18 rows in sc = 4"/10 cm square
Using K-10^1/$_2$ (6.5 mm) hook: 12 sts and 16 rows in sc = 4"/10 cm square

Notes

1. The hat is worked from the top down in rounds. If you like, you can use a stitch marker to mark the first stitch of each round for reference.
2. The ch2 at the beginning of each round does not count as a stitch.
3. See page 128 for a tutorial on Double Crochet Decrease (dc dec).

Special Techniques
Front Post Treble (fptr)

1 Yarn over 2 times, insert hook around post of stitch from front to back to front, yarn over, and pull yarn through: 4 loops on hook.

2 Yarn over, pull through first 2 loops on hook: 3 loops on hook.

(continued)

3 Yarn over, pull through 2 loops on hook: 2 loops on hook.

4 Yarn over, pull through last 2 loops on hook. Front post treble is complete.

Cable (worked over 6 stitches)

Fptr in fourth stitch from hook, fptr in fifth stitch, fptr in sixth stitch. Working in front of 3 stitches just created, fptr in first, second, and third stitches that you skipped, in that order, to complete cable.

NOTE: When moving onto the next stitch in the pattern, work in the stitch after the cable (it will be after the sixth stitch).

Hat

SMALL

Using H-8 (5.0 mm) hook and Color A, ch4.
Round 1: 8dc in fourth chain from hook, sl st to first stitch to join (8 sts).
Round 2: Ch2, * 2dc, (dc, fptr) (see Special Techniques) in next stitch, repeat from * to complete round, sl st to first stitch to join (16 sts).
Round 3: Ch2, * dc, 2dc in next stitch, dc, 2fptr in next stitch, repeat from * to complete round, sl st to first stitch to join (24 sts).

Round 4: Ch2, * dc2, 2dc in next stitch, dc, fptr, 2fptr in next stitch, repeat from * to complete round, sl st to first stitch to join (32 sts).
Round 5: Ch2, * dc5, 2fptr in next stitch, fptr, 2fptr in next stitch, repeat from * to complete round, sl st to first stitch to join (40 sts).
Round 6: Ch2, * dc5, fptr2, 2fptr in next stitch, fptr2, repeat from * to complete round, sl st to first stitch to join (44 sts).
Round 7: Ch2, * dc5, fptr6, repeat from * to complete round, sl st to first stitch to join (44 sts).
Round 8: Ch2, * dc5, Cable (see Special Techniques), repeat from * to complete round, sl st to first stitch to join.
Round 9: Ch2, * dc5, fptr6, repeat from * to complete round, sl st to first stitch to join.
Round 10: Repeat Round 8.
Round 11: Repeat Round 9.
Rounds 12–15: Ch1, sc in each stitch, sl st to first stitch to join.
Fasten off. Weave in ends.

MEDIUM

Using K-10½ (6.5 mm) hook and Color B, ch4.
Round 1: 8dc in fourth chain from hook, sl st to first stitch to join (8 sts).
Round 2: Ch2, * 2dc, (dc, fptr) (see Special Techniques) in next stitch, repeat from * to complete round, sl st to first stitch to join (16 sts).

Round 3: Ch2, * dc, 2dc in next stitch, dc, 2fptr in next stitch, repeat from * to complete round, sl st to first stitch to join (24 sts).

Round 4: Ch2, * dc2, 2dc in next stitch, dc, fptr, 2fptr in next stitch, repeat from * to complete round, sl st to first stitch to join (32 sts).

Round 5: Ch2, * dc5, 2fptr on next stitch, fptr, 2fptr in next stitch, repeat from * to complete round, sl st to first stitch to join (40 sts).

Round 6: Ch2, * dc5, fptr2, 2fptr on next stitch, fptr2, repeat from * to complete round, sl st to first stitch to join (44 sts).

Round 7: Ch2, * dc5, fptr6, repeat from * to complete round, sl st to first stitch to join.

Round 8: Ch2, * dc5, Cable (see Special Techniques), repeat from * to complete round, sl st to first stitch to join.

Round 9: Ch2, * dc5, fptr6, repeat from * to complete round, sl st to first stitch to join.

Rounds 10–13: Repeat Rounds 8 and 9 twice.

Rounds 14–17: Ch1, sc in each stitch, sl st to first stitch to join.

Fasten off. Weave in ends.

LARGE

Using K-10^1/$_2$ (6.5 mm) hook and Color A, ch4.

Round 1: 12dc in fourth chain from hook, sl st to first stitch to join (12 sts).

Round 2: Ch2, * 2dc, (dc, fptr) (see Special Techniques) in next stitch, repeat from * to complete round, sl st to first stitch to join (24 sts).

Round 3: Ch2, * dc, 2dc in next stitch, dc, 2fptr in next stitch, repeat from * to complete round, sl st to first stitch to join (36 sts).

Round 4: Ch2, * dc2, 2dc in next stitch, dc, fptr, 2fptr in next stitch, repeat from * to complete round, sl st to first stitch to join (48 sts).

Round 5: Ch2, * dc5, 2fptr in next stitch, fptr, 2fptr in next stitch, repeat from * to complete round, sl st to first stitch to join (60 sts).

Round 6: Ch2, * dc5, fptr2, 2fptr on next stitch, fptr2, repeat from * to complete round, sl st to first stitch to join (66 sts).

Round 7: Ch2, * dc5, fptr6, repeat from * to complete round, sl st to first stitch to join.

Round 8: Ch2, * dc5, Cable (see Special Techniques), repeat from * to complete round, sl st to first stitch to join.

Round 9: Ch2, * dc5, fptr6, repeat from * to complete round, sl st to first stitch to join.

Rounds 10–11: Repeat Rounds 8–9.

Round 12: Ch2, *dc dec, dc in next stitch, dc dec, fptr6, repeat from * to complete round, sl st to first stitch to join (54 sts).

Rounds 13–18: Ch1, sc in each stitch, sl st to first stitch to join.

Fasten off. Weave in ends.

I'm an Elf! Pixie

Dress up and stay warm in this fun holiday hat. Make it in a variety of colors for each member of the family! It's great for gifts, holiday family photos, and parties for all ages!

Skill Level
Beginner

Finished Measurements
Head circumference: X-Small: 12–14.5"/30.5–37 cm, Small: 15–17.5"/38–44.5 cm, Medium: 17.5–19"/44.5–48 cm, Large: 19–22.5"/48–57 cm, X-Large: 23–24.5"/58.5–62 cm

Yarn
• Red Heart Soft Yarn, medium worsted weight #4 yarn (100% acrylic; 256 yd/5 oz, 234 m/142 g per skein)
    1 skein #4420 Guacamole (Color A)
• Lion Brand Vanna's Choice, medium worsted weight #4 yarn (100% acrylic; 170 yd/3.5 oz, 155 m/100 g per skein)
    1 skein #860-180 Cranberry (Color B)
    1 skein #860-157 Radiant Yellow (Color C)

Hook and Other Materials
• 7 (4.75 mm) hook or size to obtain gauge
• Stitch marker (optional)

Gauge
14 sts and 9 rows in dc = 4"/10 cm square

Notes
1. This hat is worked from the top down continuously in the round. If you like, you can mark the first stitch of each round with a stitch marker for reference.
2. To change colors, push the hook through the last stitch of the first color, pull the yarn back through, yarn over with the NEXT color, and pull through. Color change is complete. Also see page 131 for a tutorial.
3. See page 124 for a tutorial on crocheting into the Back Loop Only (blo) and page 134 for how to make a pom-pom.

Hat

X-SMALL
Using Color A, ch4, sl st to first chain to create a ring.
Round 1: Ch2, 4dc in ring (4 sts).
Round 2: Working continuously in the round, 2dc in first stitch, dc3 (5 sts).
Round 3: 2dc in first stitch, dc4 (6 sts).
Round 4: 2dc in first stitch, dc5 (7 sts).
Round 5: 2dc in first stitch, dc6 (8 sts).

Round 6: 2dc in first stitch, dc7 (9 sts).
Round 7: 2dc in first stitch, dc8 (10 sts).
Round 8: 2dc in first stitch, dc9 (11 sts).
Round 9: 2dc in first stitch, dc10 (12 sts).
Round 10: 2dc in first stitch, dc11 (13 sts).
Round 11: 2dc in first stitch, dc12 (14 sts).
Round 12: 2dc in first stitch, dc13 (15 sts).
Round 13: 2dc in first stitch, dc14 (16 sts).
Round 14: * Dc, 2dc in next stitch, repeat from * to complete round (24 sts).
Round 15: * Dc2, 2dc in next stitch, repeat from * to complete round (32 sts).
Round 16: * Dc3, 2dc in next stitch, repeat from * to complete round (40 sts).
Rounds 17–24: Dc in each stitch.
Round 25: Drop Color A, join Color B, ch1, sc in each stitch, sl st to beginning ch to join round.
Round 26: Turn, ch1, sc in blo of each stitch.
Rounds 27–29: Working continuously in the round, sc in each stitch.
Round 30: * Sc3, (sl st, ch4, sl st) in next stitch, repeat from * to complete round, sl st to first stitch to join.
Fasten off. Weave in ends.

SMALL
Using Color A, ch4, sl st to first chain to create a ring.
Round 1: Ch2, 4dc in ring (4 sts).
Round 2: Working continuously in the round, 2dc in first stitch, dc3 (5 sts).
Round 3: 2dc in first stitch, dc4 (6 sts).
Round 4: 2dc in first stitch, dc5 (7 sts).
Round 5: 2dc in first stitch, dc6 (8 sts).
Round 6: 2dc in first stitch, dc7 (9 sts).
Round 7: 2dc in first stitch, dc8 (10 sts).
Round 8: 2dc in first stitch, dc9 (11 sts).
Round 9: 2dc in first stitch, dc10 (12 sts).
Round 10: 2dc in first stitch, dc11 (13 sts).
Round 11: 2dc in first stitch, dc12 (14 sts).
Round 12: 2dc in first stitch, dc13 (15 sts).
Round 13: 2dc in first stitch, dc14 (16 sts).
Round 14: * Dc, 2dc in next stitch, repeat from * to complete round (24 sts).
Round 15: * Dc2, 2dc in next stitch, repeat from * to complete round (32 sts).
Round 16: * Dc3, 2dc in next stitch, repeat from * to complete round (40 sts).
Round 17: * Dc4, 2dc in next stitch, repeat from * to complete round (48 sts).

Rounds 18–30: Dc in each stitch.
Round 31: Drop Color A, join Color B, ch1, sc in each stitch, sl st to beginning ch to join round.
Round 32: Turn, ch1, sc in blo of each stitch.
Rounds 33–35: Working continuously in the round, sc in each stitch.
Round 36: * Sc3, (sl st, ch4, sl st) in next stitch, repeat from * to complete round, sl st to first stitch to join.
Fasten off. Weave in ends.

MEDIUM

Using Color A, ch4, sl st to first chain to create a ring.
Round 1: Ch2, 4dc in ring (4 sts).
Round 2: Working continuously in the round, 2dc in first stitch, dc3 (5 sts).
Round 3: 2dc in first stitch, dc4 (6 sts).
Round 4: 2dc in first stitch, dc5 (7 sts).
Round 5: 2dc in first stitch, dc6 (8 sts).
Round 6: 2dc in first stitch, dc7 (9 sts).
Round 7: 2dc in first stitch, dc8 (10 sts).
Round 8: 2dc in first stitch, dc9 (11 sts).
Round 9: 2dc in first stitch, dc10 (12 sts).
Round 10: 2dc in first stitch, dc11 (13 sts).
Round 11: 2dc in first stitch, dc12 (14 sts).
Round 12: 2dc in first stitch, dc13 (15 sts).
Round 13: 2dc in first stitch, dc14 (16 sts).
Round 14: 2dc in first stitch, dc15 (17 sts).
Round 15: 2dc in first stitch, dc16 (18 sts).
Round 16: * Dc2, 2dc in next stitch, repeat from * to complete round (24 sts).
Round 17: * Dc3, 2dc in next stitch, repeat from * to complete round (30 sts).
Round 18: * Dc4, 2dc in next stitch, repeat from * to complete round (36 sts).
Round 19: * Dc5, 2dc in next stitch, repeat from * to complete round (42 sts).
Round 20: * Dc6, 2dc in next stitch, repeat from * to complete round (48 sts).
Round 21: * Dc7, 2dc in next stitch, repeat from * to complete round (54 sts).
Round 22: * Dc8, 2dc, repeat from * to complete round (60 sts).
Rounds 23–33: Dc in each stitch.
Round 34: Drop Color A, join Color B, ch1, sc in each stitch, sl st to beginning ch to join round.
Round 35: Turn, ch1, sc in blo of each stitch.
Rounds 36–38: Working continuously in the round, sc in each stitch.
Round 39: * Sc3, (sl st, ch4, sl st) in next stitch, repeat from * to complete round, sl st to first stitch to join.
Fasten off. Weave in ends.

LARGE

Using Color A, ch4, sl st to first chain to create a ring.
Round 1: Ch2, 4dc in ring (4 sts).
Round 2: Working continuously in the round, 2dc in first stitch, dc3 (5 sts).

Round 3: 2dc in first stitch, dc4 (6 sts).
Round 4: 2dc in first stitch, dc5 (7 sts).
Round 5: 2dc in first stitch, dc6 (8 sts).
Round 6: 2dc in first stitch, dc7 (9 sts).
Round 7: 2dc in first stitch, dc8 (10 sts).
Round 8: 2dc in first stitch, dc9 (11 sts).
Round 9: 2dc in first stitch, dc10 (12 sts).
Round 10: 2dc in first stitch, dc11 (13 sts).
Round 11: 2dc in first stitch, dc12 (14 sts).
Round 12: 2dc in first stitch, dc13 (15 sts).
Round 13: 2dc in first stitch, dc14 (16 sts).
Round 14: 2dc in first stitch, dc15 (17 sts).
Round 15: 2dc in first stitch, dc16 (18 sts).
Round 16: 2dc in first stitch, dc17 (19 sts).
Round 17: 2dc in first stitch, dc18 (20 sts).
Round 18: * Dc3, 2dc in next stitch, repeat from * to complete round (25 sts).
Round 19: * Dc4, 2dc in next stitch, repeat from * to complete round (30 sts).
Round 20: * Dc2, 2dc in next stitch, repeat from * to complete round (40 sts).
Round 21: * Dc3, 2dc in next stitch, repeat from * to complete round (50 sts).
Round 22: * Dc4, 2dc in next stitch, repeat from * to complete round (60 sts).
Round 23: * Dc5, 2dc in next stitch, repeat from * to complete round (70 sts).
Rounds 24–33: Dc in each stitch.

Round 34: Drop Color A, join Color B, ch1, sc in each stitch, sl st to beginning ch to join round.

Round 35: Turn, ch1, sc in blo of each stitch.

Rounds 36–38: Working continuously in the round, sc in each stitch.

Round 39: * Sc4, (sl st, ch4, sl st) in next stitch, repeat from * to complete round, sl st to first stitch to join.

Fasten off. Weave in ends.

X-LARGE

Using Color A, ch4, sl st to first chain to create a ring.

Round 1: Ch2, 4dc in ring (4 sts).

Round 2: Working continuously in the round, 2dc in first stitch, dc3 (5 sts).

Round 3: 2dc in first stitch, dc4 (6 sts).

Round 4: 2dc in first stitch, dc5 (7 sts).

Round 5: 2dc in first stitch, dc6 (8 sts).

Round 6: 2dc in first stitch, dc7 (9 sts).

Round 7: 2dc in first stitch, dc8 (10 sts).

Round 8: 2dc in first stitch, dc9 (11 sts).

Round 9: 2dc in first stitch, dc10 (12 sts).

Round 10: 2dc in first stitch, dc11 (13 sts).

Round 11: 2dc in first stitch, dc12 (14 sts).

Round 12: 2dc in first stitch, dc13 (15 sts).

Round 13: 2dc in first stitch, dc14 (16 sts).

Round 14: 2dc in first stitch, dc15 (17 sts).

Round 15: 2dc in first stitch, dc16 (18 sts).

Round 16: 2dc in first stitch, dc17 (19 sts).

Round 17: 2dc in first stitch, dc18 (20 sts).

Round 18: * Dc3, 2dc in next stitch, repeat from * to complete round (25 sts).

Round 19: * Dc4, 2dc in next stitch, repeat from * to complete round (30 sts).

Round 20: * Dc2, 2dc in next stitch, repeat from * to complete round (40 sts).

Round 21: * Dc3, 2dc in next stitch, repeat from * to complete round (50 sts).

Round 22: * Dc4, 2dc in next stitch, repeat from * to complete round (60 sts).

Round 23: * Dc5, 2dc in next stitch, repeat from * to complete round (70 sts).

Round 24: * Dc6, 2dc in next stitch, repeat from * to complete round (80 sts).

Rounds 25–35: Dc in each stitch.

Round 36: Drop Color A, join Color B, ch1, sc in each stitch, sl st to beginning ch to join round.

Round 37: Turn, ch1, sc in blo of each stitch.

Rounds 38–40: Working continuously in the round, sc in each stitch.

Round 41: * Sc4, (sl st, ch4, sl st) in next stitch, repeat from * to complete round, sl st to first stitch to join.

Fasten off. Weave in ends.

Finishing

Make 1 pom-pom in Color C and attach to top of hat.

Sock Monkey Twist

Turn up the color and style with this playful twist on the sock monkey.

Skill Level
Beginner

Finished Measurements
Head circumference: Small: 15–17.5"/38–44.5 cm, Medium: 17.5–19"/44.5–48 cm, Large: 19–22.5"/48–57 cm, X-Large: 23–24.5"/58.5–62 cm
Height: Small: 6–6.5"/15–16.5 cm, Medium: 6.5–7"/16.5–18 cm, Large: 7–7.5"/18–19 cm, X-Large: 7.5–8"/19–20 cm

Yarn
- Lion Brand Vanna's Choice, medium worsted weight #4 yarn (100% acrylic; 170 yd/3.5 oz, 155m/100 g per skein)
    1 skein #860-123 Beige (Color A)
    1 skein #860-143 Antique Rose (Color B)
    1 skein #860-158 Mustard (Color C)
    1 skein #860- White (Color D)
- Red Heart Soft Yarn, medium worsted weight #4 yarn (100% acrylic; 256 yd/5 oz, 234 m/142 g per skein)
    1 skein #4420 Guacamole (Color E)
    1 skein #3729 Grape Raisin UVA (Color F)

Hook and Other Materials
- H-8 (5.0 mm) hook or size needed to obtain gauge
- Stitch marker (optional)
- Yarn needle
- 2 medium black buttons
- Sewing thread and needle

Gauge
15 sts and 12 rows in hdc = 4"/10 cm square

Notes
1. You will make the hat, earflaps, and ties first. The ears, eyes, mouth, and flower will be added separately.
2. The hat is worked from the top down continuously in the round. If you like, you can mark the first stitch of each round with a stitch marker for reference.
3. To change colors, push the hook through the last stitch of the first color, pull the yarn back through, yarn over with the NEXT color, and pull through. Color change is complete. Also see page 131 for a tutorial.
4. See page 126 for a tutorial on Single Crochet Decrease (sc dec) and page 131 for Treble Crochet (tr).

Special Techniques
Front Post Single Crochet (fpsc)

1 Insert hook around the post from front to back to front (see Anatomy of a Stitch on page 124 for where the post is located).

2 Yarn over and pull yarn back around post: 2 loops on hook.

3 Yarn over and draw yarn through 2 loops on hook to complete.

Hat

SMALL

Using Color A, ch4, sl st to first chain to create a ring.
Round 1: Ch2 (counts as hdc), 7hdc in ring (8 sts).
Round 2: Working continuously in the round, 2hdc in each stitch (16 sts).
Round 3: * Hdc, 2hdc in next stitch, repeat from * to complete round (24 sts).
Round 4: * Hdc2, 2hdc in next stitch, repeat from * to complete round (32 sts).
Round 5: * Hdc3, 2hdc in next stitch, repeat from * to complete round (40 sts).
Round 6: * Hdc4, 2hdc in next stitch, repeat from * to complete round (48 sts).
Rounds 7–8: Hdc in each stitch.
Round 9: Fasten off Color A, join Color B, hdc in each stitch.
Rounds 10–12: Hdc in each stitch.
Round 13: Fasten off Color B, join Color F, hdc in each stitch.
Rounds 14–16: Hdc in each stitch.
Round 17: Fasten off Color F, join Color E, hdc in each stitch.
Rounds 18–20: Hdc in each stitch. To finish, sl st to first stitch of round to join.
Fasten off. Weave in ends.

MEDIUM

Using Color A, ch4, sl st to first chain to create a ring.
Round 1: Ch2 (counts as hdc), 8hdc in ring (9 sts).
Round 2: Working continuously in the round, 2hdc in each stitch (18 sts).
Round 3: * Hdc, 2hdc in next stitch, repeat from * to complete round (27 sts).
Round 4: * Hdc2, 2hdc in next stitch, repeat from * to complete round (36 sts).
Round 5: * Hdc3, 2hdc in next stitch, repeat from * to complete round (45 sts).
Round 6: * Hdc4, 2hdc in next stitch, repeat from * to complete round (54 sts).
Rounds 7–8: * Hdc in each stitch.
Round 9: Fasten off Color A, join Color B, hdc in each stitch.
Rounds 10–11: Hdc in each stitch.
Round 12: Fasten off Color B, join Color F, hdc in each stitch.
Rounds 13–16: Hdc in each stitch.
Round 17: Fasten off Color F, join Color E, hdc in each stitch.
Rounds 18–22: Hdc in each stitch. To finish, sl st to first stitch of round to join.
Fasten off. Weave in ends.

LARGE

Using Color A, ch4, sl st to first chain to create a ring.
Round 1: Ch2 (counts as hdc), 10hdc in ring (11 sts).
Round 2: Working continuously in the round, 2hdc in each stitch (22 sts).
Round 3: * Hdc, 2hdc in next stitch, repeat from * to complete round (33 sts).
Round 4: * Hdc2, 2hdc in next stitch, repeat from * to complete round (44 sts).

Round 5: * Hdc3, 2hdc in next stitch, repeat from * to complete round (55 sts).
Round 6: * Hdc4, 2hdc in next stitch, repeat from * to complete round (66 sts).
Round 7: Hdc in each stitch.
Round 8: Fasten off Color A, join Color B, hdc in each stitch.
Rounds 9–13: Hdc in each stitch.
Round 14: Fasten off Color B, join Color F, hdc in each stitch.
Rounds 15–20: Hdc in each stitch.
Round 21: Fasten off Color F, join Color E, hdc in each stitch.
Rounds 22–25: Hdc in each stitch. To finish, sl st to first stitch of round to join.
Fasten off. Weave in ends.

X-LARGE

Using Color A, ch4, sl st to first chain to create a ring.
Round 1: Ch2 (counts as hdc), 11hdc in ring (12 sts).
Round 2: Working continuously in the round, 2hdc in each stitch (24 sts).
Round 3: * Hdc, 2hdc in next stitch, repeat from * to complete round (36 sts).
Round 4: * Hdc2, 2hdc in next stitch, repeat from * to complete round (48 sts).
Round 5: * Hdc3, 2hdc in next stitch, repeat from * to complete round (60 sts).
Round 6: * Hdc4, 2hdc in next stitch, repeat from * to complete round (72 sts).
Round 7: Hdc in each stitch.
Round 8: Fasten off Color A, join Color B, hdc in each stitch.
Rounds 9–13: Hdc in each stitch.
Round 14: Fasten off Color B, join Color F, hdc in each stitch.
Rounds 15–20: Hdc in each stitch.
Round 21: Fasten off Color F, join Color E, hdc in each stitch.
Rounds 22–25: Hdc in each stitch. To finish, sl st to first stitch of round to join. Fasten off. Weave in ends.

Earflaps (make 2)

Fold hat in half and mark opposite sides on last round with stitch markers. Join Color E at a marker and follow pattern per size to complete earflaps.

SMALL & MEDIUM

Using Color E, ch1.
Row 1: 8sc (8 sts).
Rows 2–6: Turn, ch1, sc to end of row.
Row 7: Turn, sc dec, sc4, sc dec (6 sts).
Row 8: Turn, sc dec, sc2, sc dec (4 sts).
Fasten off. Weave in ends.
Repeat for flap on opposite side.

LARGE & X-LARGE

Using Color E, ch1.
Row 1: 10sc (10 sts).
Rows 2–7: Turn, ch1, sc to end of row.
Row 8: Turn, sc dec, sc6, sc dec (8 sts).
Row 9: Turn, sc dec, sc4, sc dec (6 sts).
Fasten off. Weave in ends.
Repeat for flap on opposite side.

TRIM (ALL SIZES)

Join Color C in last stitch of beanie where it meets one of the ear flaps.
Row 1: Ch1, fpsc in each stitch around beanie and in all row ends around earflaps. Sl st to beginning ch to join.
Fasten off. Weave in ends.

Ties (make 2)

Cut 6 lengths of yarn 3'/1 m long. Align ends, then, holding the strands together, fold them in half. With a crochet hook, pull center fold through center of end of earflap. Take hold of the cut ends and thread them through the fold. Pull tight. Working with 3 groups of 4 strands each, braid ties. Knot the ends and trim to finish.

The lengths of yarn for each tie are threaded through the center edge of the earflap, then braided.

Ears (make 2)

Using Color B, ch2.
Round 1: Sc6 in second chain from hook.
Round 2: Turn, ch1, 2sc in each stitch (12 sts).
Round 3: Turn, ch1, * sc, 2sc in next stitch, repeat from * to complete round (18 sts).
Fasten off, leaving a long tail to sew onto hat.

Mouth

SMALL & MEDIUM

Using Color D, ch12.
Round 1: Turn, sc10, 4sc in last chain; working on opposite side of chain, sc9, 3sc in last chain, sl st to first stitch to join (26 sts).
Fasten off, leaving a long tail to sew onto hat.

LARGE & X-LARGE

Using Color D, ch21.
Round 1: Turn, sc19, 4sc in last chain; working on opposite side of chain, sc18, 3sc in last chain, sl st to first stitch to join (44).
Fasten off, leaving a long tail to sew onto hat.

Large Flower

Using Color C, ch4, sl st to first chain to create a ring.
Round 1: Ch1, 8sc in ring, sl st to first chain to join (8 sts).
Round 2: Ch1, * (sl st, ch1, dc, 2tr, dc, ch1, sl st) in next stitch, repeat from * to complete round, sl st to ch1 to join (8 petals).
Fasten off. Weave in ends.

Small Flower

Using Color C, ch4, sl st to first chain to create a ring .
Round 1: Ch1, 6 sc in ring, sl st to first chain to join (6 sts).
Round 2: Ch1, * (sl st, ch1, dc3, ch1, sl st) in next stitch, repeat from * to complete round, sl st to ch1 to join (6 petals).
Fasten off. Weave in ends.

Finishing

Using yarn needle, attach mouth, sewing around last round. Using Color B, join yarn at first chain of the last round and sl st loosely across center of mouth. Fasten off. Weave in ends.

Using yarn needle, attach ears at sides of hat. Sew large button above one ear. Slip large flower over button, then small flower.

Using sewing needles and thread, sew two black buttons onto hat for eyes to finish.

Groovy Waves Beanie

You found me! I couldn't resist snuggling with one of my own little kiddos in this fun hat! It is fun to crochet and see the pattern appear in these cool waves!

Skill Level
Beginner

Finished Measurements
Head circumference: Small: 15–17.5"/38–44.5 cm, Medium: 17.5–19"/44.5–48 cm, Large: 19–22.5"/48–57 cm. X-Large: 23–24.5"/58.5–62 cm
Height: Small: 6–6.5"/15–16.5 cm, Medium: 6.5–7"/16.5–18 cm, Large: 7–7.5"/18–19 cm, X-Large: 7.5–8"/19–20.5 cm

Yarn
• Red Heart Soft Yarn, medium worsted weight #4 yarn (100% acrylic; 256 yd/5 oz, 234 m/142 g per skein)
   1 skein #3729 Grape (Color A) (for Large & X-Large only)
   1 skein #9010 Charcoal (Color B)
   1 skein #4601 Off White (Color C)
   1 skein #9925 Really Red (Color D) (for Small & Medium only)

Hook and Other Materials
• H-8 (5.0 mm) hook or size needed to obtain gauge
• J-10 (6.0 mm) hook or size needed to obtain gauge (for X-Large only)
• Stitch marker (optional)

Gauge
Using H-8 (5.0 mm) hook, 12 sts and 6 rows in dc = 3"/7.5 cm square
Using J-10 (6.0 mm) hook, 10 sts and 4 rows in dc = 3"/7.5 cm square

Notes
1. The beanie is worked from the top down, working continuously in the round from Round 8 on. If you like, you can mark the first stitch of each round with a stitch marker for reference.
2. The ch2 at the beginning of the rounds does not count as a stitch.
3. When you change colors, you will carry the old yarn, instead of fastening it off. That will allow you to simply pick the yarn up later with no ends to weave in. For a tutorial, see page 132.
4. To change colors, push the hook through the last stitch of the first color, pull the yarn back through, yarn over with the NEXT color, and pull through. Color change is complete. Also see page 131 for a tutorial.

Special Techniques
Reverse Single Crochet (rev sc)

1 With right side facing you, insert hook front to back in stitch to the right. In the photo above, the hook is pointing to the next stitch to be worked. (The hook has been removed from the working loop so the loop does not get in the way of showing the stitch. Do not remove the hook from the loop when you work their stitch.)

2 Yarn over and pull yarn through stitch—2 loops on hook.

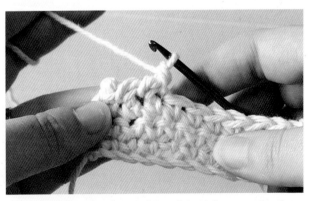

3 Yarn over and pull yarn through both loops on hook to complete the stitch.

Hat

SMALL

Using H-8 (5.0 mm) hook and Color D, ch4.

Round 1: 8dc in fourth chain from hook, sl st to first stitch to join round (8 sts).

Round 2: Ch2, 2dc in each stitch, sl st to first stitch to join (16 sts).

Round 3: Ch2, * dc, 2dc in next stitch, repeat from * to complete round, sl st to first stitch to join (24 sts).

Round 4: Ch2, * dc2, 2dc in next stitch, repeat from * to complete round, sl st to first stitch to join (32 sts).

Round 5: Ch2, * dc3, 2dc in next stitch, repeat from * to complete round, sl st to first stitch to join (40 sts).

Round 6: Ch2, * dc4, 2dc in next stitch, repeat from * to complete round, sl st to first stitch to join (48 sts).

Round 7: Drop Color D, join Color B, ch1, * sc3, hdc2, dc5, hdc2, repeat from * to complete round, sl st to first stitch to join.

Round 8: Working continuously in the round, * sc3, hdc2, dc5, hdc2, repeat from * to complete round.

Round 9: Drop Color B, join Color C, sc in each stitch.

Round 10: Drop Color C, pick up Color D, * dc4, hdc2, sc3, hdc2, dc, repeat from * to complete round.

Round 11: * Dc4, hdc2, sc3, hdc2, dc, repeat from * to complete round.

Round 12: Drop Color D, pick up Color C, sc in each stitch.

Round 13: Drop Color C, pick up Color B, * sc3, hdc2, dc5, hdc2, repeat from * to complete round.

Round 14: * Sc3, hdc2, dc5, hdc2, repeat from * to complete round.

Round 15: Drop Color B, pick up Color C, sc in each stitch.

Round 16: Repeat Round 10.

Round 17: Repeat Round 12.

Round 18: * Sc6, sc dec, repeat from * to complete round (42 sts).

Round 19: Sc in each stitch.

Round 20: Drop Color C, pick up Color D, rev sc (see Special Technique) in each st around, sl st to first stitch to join. Fasten off. Weave in ends.

Close-up of the wave pattern.

MEDIUM

Using H-8 (5.0 mm) hook and Color D, ch4.

Round 1: 10dc in fourth chain from hook, sl st to first stitch to join round (10 sts).

Round 2: Ch2, 2dc in each stitch, sl st to first stitch to join (20 sts).

Round 3: Ch2, * dc, 2dc in next stitch, repeat from * to complete round, sl st to first stitch to join (30 sts).

Round 4: Ch2, * dc2, 2dc in next stitch, repeat from * to complete round, sl st to first stitch to join (40 sts).

Round 5: Ch2, * dc3, 2dc in next stitch, repeat from * to complete round, sl st to first stitch to join (50 sts).

Round 6: Ch2, * dc4, 2dc in next stitch, repeat from * to complete round, sl st to first stitch to join (60 sts).

Round 7: Drop Color D, join Color B, * sc3, hdc2, dc5, hdc2, repeat from * to complete round, sl st to first stitch to join.

Round 8: Working continuously in the round, * sc3, hdc2, dc5, hdc2, repeat from * to complete round.

Round 9: Drop Color B, join Color C, sc in each stitch.

Round 10: Drop Color C, pick up Color D, * dc4, hdc2, sc3, hdc2, dc, repeat from * to complete round.

Round 11: * Dc4, hdc2, sc3, hdc2, dc, repeat from * to complete round.

Round 12: Drop Color D, pick up Color C, sc in each stitch.

Round 13: Drop Color C, pick up Color B, * sc3, hdc2, dc5, hdc2, repeat from * to complete round.

Round 14: * Sc3, hdc2, dc5, hdc2, repeat from * to complete round.

Round 15: Drop Color B, pick up Color C, sc in each stitch.

Rounds 16–19: Repeat Rounds 10–13.

Round 20: Repeat Round 15.

Round 21: * Sc8, sc dec, repeat from * to complete round (54 sts).

Round 22: Sc in each stitch.

Round 23: Drop Color C, pick up Color D, rev sc (see Special Technique) in each st around, sl st to first stitch to join. Fasten off. Weave in ends.

LARGE

Using H-8 (5.0 mm) hook and Color A, ch4.

Round 1: 12dc in fourth chain from hook, sl st to first stitch to join round (12 sts).

Round 2: Ch2, 2dc in each stitch, sl st to first stitch to join (24 sts).

Round 3: Ch2, * dc, 2dc in next stitch, repeat from * to complete round, sl st to first stitch to join (36 sts).

Round 4: Ch2, * dc2, 2dc in next stitch, repeat from * to complete round, sl st to first stitch to join (48 sts).

Round 5: Ch2, * dc3, 2dc in next stitch, repeat from * to complete round, sl st to first stitch to join (60 sts).

Round 6: Ch2, * dc4, 2dc in next stitch, repeat from * to complete round, sl st to first stitch to join (72 sts).

Round 7: Drop Color D, join Color B, * sc3, hdc2, dc5, hdc2, repeat from * to complete round, sl st to first stitch to join.

Round 8: Working continuously in the round, * sc3, hdc2, dc5, hdc2, repeat from * to complete round.

Round 9: Drop Color B, join Color C, sc in each stitch.

Round 10: Drop Color C, pick up Color D, * dc4, hdc2, sc3, hdc2, dc, repeat from * to complete round.

Round 11: * Dc4, hdc2, sc3, hdc2, dc, repeat from * to complete round.

Round 12: Drop Color D, pick up Color C, sc in each stitch.

Round 13: Drop Color C, pick up Color B, * sc3, hdc2, dc5, hdc2, repeat from * to complete round.

Round 14: * Sc3, hdc2, dc5, hdc2, repeat from * to complete round.

Round 15: Drop Color B, pick up Color C, sc in each stitch.

Rounds 16–19: Repeat Rounds 10–13.

Round 20: Repeat Round 15.

Round 21: * Sc4, sc dec, repeat from * to complete round (60 sts).

Round 22: Sc in each stitch.

Round 23: Drop Color C, pick up Color D, rev sc (see Special Technique) in each st around, sl st to first stitch to join. Fasten off. Weave in ends.

X-LARGE

Using J-10 (6.0 mm) hook, work the Large pattern. The larger hook will naturally increase the gauge and finished size.

Ocean Air Cloche

This hat is the perfect accessory for a trip to the beach or an outdoor event. Light and airy, it adds flair to any outfit. The large flower provides pizzazz that kids, moms, and grandmas will all appreciate.

Skill Level
Intermediate

Finished Measurements
Head circumference: Small: 15–17.5"/38.44.5 cm, Medium: 17.5–19"/44.5–48 cm, Large: 19–22.5"/48–57 cm
Height: Small: 6–6.5"/15–16.5, Medium: 6.5–7"/16.5–18 cm, Large: 7–7.5"/18–19 cm

Yarn
- Patons Silk Bamboo, light weight #3 yarn (70% viscose from bamboo/30% silk; 102 yd/2.2 oz, 93 m/62g per skein)
  2 skeins #85219 Sea

Hook and Other Materials
- F-5 (3.75 mm) hook or size to obtain gauge
- Yarn needle

Gauge
18 sts and 10 rows in dc = 4"/10 cm square

Notes
1. The hat is worked from the top down.
2. The trim and flower are created on the last row. You will roll up the flower and, using the yarn needle, sew it onto the hat to finish.
3. The ch4 at the beginning of rounds counts as the first dc and ch1; the ch3 counts as the first dc.
4. The ch2 at the beginning of rounds does not count as a stitch.

Hat

SMALL
Ch4.
Round 1: * (Dc, ch1) 8 times in fourth chain from hook, sl st to first stitch to join (16 sts).
Round 2: Ch4, * (dc, ch1) in each stitch, sl st to third chain of first ch4 to join (32 sts).
Round 3: Ch3, (dc, ch1) in next stitch, * dc, (dc, ch1) in next stitch, repeat from * to complete round, sl st to third chain of first ch3 to join (48 sts).
Round 4: Ch4, skip 1 stitch, (dc, ch1) in next stitch, * (dc, ch1) in next stitch, skip 1 stitch, (dc, ch1) in next stitch, repeat from * to complete round, sl st to third chain of first ch4 to join (64 sts).
Round 5: Ch4, skip 1 stitch, (dc, ch1) in next stitch, dc, * (dc, ch1) in next stitch, skip 1 stitch, (dc, ch1) in next stitch, dc, repeat from * to complete round, sl st to third chain of first ch4 to join (80 sts).
Round 6: Ch4, * dc in next ch1 space, ch1, repeat from * to complete round, sl st to first stitch to join.
Round 7: Ch2, dc in first ch1 space, ch1, * dc in next ch1 space, ch1, repeat from * to complete round, sl st to first dc to join.
Rounds 8–11: Repeat Rounds 6 and 7 twice.
Round 12: Repeat Round 6.
Round 13: Ch2, dc in first ch1 space, ch1, * dc in next ch1 space, ch1, repeat from * to complete round, ch67 (147 sts).
NOTE: The ch67 will be will be used to create the flower.
Row 14: Turn, dc in third ch from hook and in each chain, dc in each stitch to complete row (145 sts).
Row 15: Turn, ch1, * skip 2 stitches, 5dc in next stitch, skip 2 stitches, sl st in next stitch, repeat from * to complete row (145 sts).
Fasten off. Weave in ends.

MEDIUM
Ch4.
Round 1: * (Dc, ch1) 8 times in fourth chain from hook, sl st to first stitch to join (16 sts).
Round 2: Ch4, * (dc, ch1) in each stitch, sl st to third chain of the first ch4 to join (32 sts).
Round 3: Ch3, (dc, ch1) in next stitch, * dc, (dc, ch1) in next stitch, repeat from * to complete round, sl st to third chain of first ch3 to join (48 sts).

Round 4: Ch4, skip 1 stitch, (dc, ch1) in next stitch, * (dc, ch1), skip 1 stitch, (dc, ch1) in next stitch, repeat from * to complete round, sl st to third chain of first ch4 to join (64 sts).

Round 5: Ch4, skip 1 stitch, (dc, ch1) in next stitch, dc, * (dc, ch1) in next stitch, skip 1 stitch, (dc, ch1) in next stitch, dc, repeat from * to complete round, sl st to third chain of first ch4 to join (80 sts).

Round 6: Ch4, skip 1 stitch, (dc, ch1) in next stitch, * (dc, ch1) in next stitch, skip1 stitch, (dc, ch1) in next stitch, repeat from * to complete round, sl st to third chain of first ch4 to join (96 sts).

Round 7: Ch4, * dc in next ch1 space, ch1, repeat from * to complete round, sl st to third chain of first ch4 to join.

Round 8: Ch2, dc in first ch1 space, ch1, * dc in next ch1 space, ch1, repeat from * to complete round, sl st to first dc to join.

Rounds 9–14: Repeat Rounds 7 and 8 three times.

Round 15: Repeat Round 7.

Round 16: Ch2, dc in first ch1 space, ch1, *dc in next ch1 space, ch1, repeat from * to complete round, ch96 (182 sts). NOTE: The ch96 will be used to create the flower.

Row 17: Turn, dc in third ch from hook and in each chain, sc in each stitch to complete row (180 sts).

Row 18: Turn, ch1, * skip 2 stitches, 5dc in next stitch, skip 2 stitches, sl st in next stitch, repeat from * to complete row (180 sts).

Fasten off. Weave in ends.

LARGE

Ch4.

Round 1: * (Dc, ch1) 8 times in fourth chain from hook, sl st to first stitch to join (16 sts).

Round 2: Ch4, * (dc, ch1) in each stitch, sl st to third chain of first ch4 to join (32 sts).

Round 3: Ch3, (dc, ch1) in next stitch, * dc, (dc, ch1) in next stitch, repeat from * to complete round, sl st to to third chain of first ch3 to join (48 sts).

Round 4: Ch4, skip 1 stitch, (dc, ch1) in next stitch, * (dc, ch1), skip 1 stitch, (dc, ch1) in next stitch, repeat from * to complete round, sl st to third chain of first ch4 to join (64 sts).

Round 5: Ch4, skip 1 stitch, (dc, ch1) in next stitch, dc, * (dc, ch1) in next stitch, skip 1 stitch, (dc, ch1) in next stitch, dc, repeat from * to complete round, sl st to third chain of first ch4 to join (80 sts).

Round 6: Ch4, skip 1 stitch, (dc, ch1) in next stitch, * (dc, ch1) in next stitch, skip1 stitch, (dc, ch1) in next stitch, repeat from * to complete round, sl st to third chain of first ch4 to join (96 sts).

Round 7: Ch4, skip 1 stitch, (dc, ch1) in next stitch, skip 1 stitch, (dc, ch1) in next stitch, (dc, ch1) in next stitch, * (dc, ch1) in next stitch, skip 1 stitch, (dc, ch1) in next stitch, skip 1 stitch, (dc, ch1) in next stitch, (dc, ch1) in next stitch), repeat from * to complete round, sl st to third chain of first ch4 to join, (112 sts).

Round 8: Ch4, * dc in next ch1 space, ch1, repeat from * to complete round, sl st to third chain of the ch4 to join.

Round 9: Ch2, dc in first ch1 space, ch1, * dc in next ch1 space, ch1, repeat from * to complete round, sl st to first dc to join.

Rounds 10–15: Repeat Rounds 8 and 9 three times.

Round 16: Repeat Round 8.

Round 17: Ch4, * dc in next ch1 space, ch1, repeat from * to complete round, ch95 (207 sts).

NOTE: The ch95 will be used to create the flower.

Row 18: Turn, dc in third ch from hook and in each chain, sc in each stitch to complete row (205 sts).

Row 19: Turn, ch1, * skip 2 stitches, 5dc in next stitch, skip 2 stitches, sl st in next stitch, repeat from * to complete row (205 sts).

Fasten off. Weave in ends.

Finishing

Roll long attachment into a flower and, using the yarn needle, sew onto hat. Fasten off. Weave in ends.

Daddy's
Bearded
Dude
Beanie

Skip your scarf or ski-mask and grab this hilarious bearded hat for chilly days! Great for the guys (and daring gals) in your life!

Skill Level

Beginner

Finished Measurements

Head circumference: Small: 15–17.5"/38–44.5 cm, Medium: 17.5–19"/44.5–48 cm, Large: 19–22.5"/48–57 cm, X-Large: 23–24.5"/58.5–62 cm
Height: Small: 6–6.5"/15–16.5 cm, Medium: 6.5–7"/16.5–18 cm, Large: 7–7.5"18–19 cm, X-Large: 7.5–8"/19–20.5 cm

Yarn

- Lion Brand Jiffy Yarn, bulky weight #5 yarn (100% acrylic; 135 yd/3 oz, 123 m/85 g per skein)
    1 skein #450-159 Dark Gray Heather (Color A)
    1 skein #450-132 Apple Green (Color B)
    1 skein #450-126 Espresso (Color C)

Hook and Other Materials

- H-8 (5.0 mm) hook or size to obtain gauge
- J-10 (6.0 mm) hook or size to obtain gauge (for X-Large size only)
- Yarn needle

Gauge

Using H-8 (5.0 mm) hook: 12 sts and 8 rows in dc = 4"/10 cm square
Using J-10 (6.0 mm) hook: 10 sts and 7 rows in dc = 4"/10 cm square

Notes

1. The beanie is worked from the top down in rounds. The beard is made separately and then sewn onto the beanie.
2. The ch1 or ch2 at the beginning of rounds does not count as a stitch.
3. When changing colors, you will carry the old yarn, instead of fastening it off. That will allow you to simply pick the yarn up later, with no ends to weave in. For a tutorial, see page 132.
4. To change colors, push the hook through the last stitch of the first color, pull the yarn back through, yarn over with the NEXT color, and pull through. Color change is complete. Also see page 131 for a tutorial.
5. See page 129 for a tutorial on Front Post Double Crochet (fpdc), page 130 on Back Post Double Crochet (bpdc), and page 131 on Treble Crochet (tr).

Hat

SMALL

Using H-8 (5.0 mm) hook and Color A, ch4.
Round 1: 8dc in fourth chain from hook, sl st to first stitch to join round (8 sts).
Round 2: Ch2, 2dc in each stitch, sl st to first stitch to join (16 sts).
Round 3: Ch2, * dc, 2dc in next stitch, repeat from * to complete round, sl st to first stitch to join (24 sts).
Round 4: Ch2, * dc2, 2dc in next stitch, repeat from * to complete round, sl st to first stitch to join (32 sts).
Round 5: Ch2, * dc3, 2dc in next stitch, repeat from * to complete round, sl st to first stitch to join (40 sts).
Round 6: Ch2, dc in each stitch, sl st to first stitch to join round.
Round 7: Drop Color A, join Color B, ch1, sc in each stitch, sl st to first stitch to join.
Round 8: Drop Color B, pick up Color A, ch2, dc in each stitch, sl st to first stitch to join.
Round 9: Drop Color A, pick up Color B, ch1, sc in each stitch, sl st to first stitch to join.
Rounds 10–11: Repeat Rounds 8 and 9.
Round 12: Repeat Round 8.
Rounds 13–15: Ch2, * fpdc, bpdc, repeat from * to complete round, sl st to first stitch to join.
Fasten off. Weave in ends.

MEDIUM

Using H-8 (5.0 mm) hook and Color A, ch4.
Round 1: 10dc in fourth chain from hook, sl st to first stitch to join round (10 sts).
Round 2: Ch2, 2dc in each stitch, sl st to first stitch to join round (20 sts).
Round 3: Ch2, * dc, 2dc in next stitch, repeat from * to complete round, sl st to first stitch to join (30 sts).
Round 4: Ch2, * dc2, 2dc in next stitch, repeat from * to complete round, sl st to first stitch to join (40 sts).
Round 5: Ch2, * dc3, 2dc in next stitch, repeat from * to complete round, sl st to first stitch to join (50 sts).
Round 6: Ch2, dc in each stitch, sl st to first stitch to join round (50 sts).
Round 7: Drop Color A, join Color B, ch1, sc in each stitch, sl st to first stitch to join.
Round 8: Drop Color B, pick up Color A, ch2, dc in each stitch, sl st to first stitch to join.
Round 9: Drop Color A, pick up Color B, ch1, sc in each stitch, sl st to first stitch to join.
Rounds 10–13: Repeat Rounds 8 and 9 twice.

Round 14: Repeat Round 8.
Rounds 15–17: Ch2, * fpdc, bpdc, repeat from * to complete round, sl st to first stitch to join.
Fasten off. Weave in ends.

LARGE

Using H-8 (5.0 mm) hook and Color A, ch4.
Round 1: 12dc in fourth chain from hook, sl st to first stitch to join round (12 sts).
Round 2: Ch2, 2dc in each stitch, sl st to first stitch to join (24 sts).
Round 3: Ch2, * dc, 2dc in next stitch, repeat from * to complete round, sl st to first stitch to join (36 sts).
Round 4: Ch2, * dc2, 2dc in next stitch, repeat from * to complete round, sl st to first stitch to join (48 sts).
Round 5: Ch2, * dc3, 2dc in next stitch, repeat from * to complete round, sl st to first stitch to join (60 sts).
Rounds 6–9: Ch2, dc in each stitch, sl st to first stitch to join round.
Round 10: Drop Color A, join Color B, ch1, sc in each stitch, sl st to first stitch to join.
Round 11: Drop Color B, pick up Color A, ch2, dc in each stitch, sl st to first stitch to join.
Round 12: Drop Color A, pick up Color B, ch1, sc in each stitch, sl st to first stitch to join.

Rounds 13–16: Repeat Rounds 11 and 12 twice.
Round 17: Drop Color B, pick up Color A, ch2, dc in each stitch, sl st to first stitch to join.
Rounds 18–20: Ch2, * fpdc, bpdc, repeat from * to complete round, sl st to first stitch to join.
Fasten off. Weave in ends.

X-LARGE

Using J-10 (6.0 mm) hook, follow the Large size pattern to complete hat. The larger hook will naturally increase the gauge and size of hat.

Beard

SMALL

Using H-8 (5.0 mm) hook and Color C, ch25.
Row 1: Sc in second chain from hook and in each chain across (24 sts).
Rows 2–5: Turn, * sc, tr, repeat from * to complete row.
Row 6: Turn, * sc, tr, repeat from * 3 more times, ch8, skip 8 stitches, * sc, tr, repeat from * to complete row.
Row 7: Turn, * sc, tr, repeat from * to complete row.
Fasten off. Weave in ends.

MEDIUM

Using H-8 (5.0 mm) hook and Color C, ch29.

Row 1: Sc in second chain from hook and in each chain across (28 sts).

Rows 2–7: Turn, * sc, tr, repeat from * to complete row (28 sts).

Row 8: Turn, * sc, tr, repeat from * 4 more times, ch8, skip 8 stitches, * sc, tr, repeat from * to complete row.

Row 9: Turn, * sc, tr, repeat from * to complete row. Fasten off. Weave in ends.

LARGE

Using H-8 (5.0 mm) hook and Color C, ch33.

Row 1: Sc in second chain from hook and in each chain across (32 sts).

Rows 2–8: Turn, * sc, tr, repeat from * to complete row (32 sts).

Row 9: Turn, * sc, tr, repeat from * 5 more times, ch8, skip 8 stitches, * sc, tr, repeat from * to complete row.

Row 10: Turn, * sc, tr, repeat from * to complete row. Fasten off. Weave in ends.

X-LARGE

Using H-8 (5.0 mm) hook and Color C, ch37.

Row 1: Sc in second chain from hook and in each chain across (36 sts).

Rows 2–8: Turn, * sc, tr, repeat from * to complete row.

Row 9: Turn, * sc, tr, repeat from * 6 more times, ch8, skip 8 stitches, * sc, tr, repeat from * to complete row.

Row 10: Turn, * sc, tr, repeat from * to complete row. Fasten off. Weave in ends.

Finishing

Using yarn needle and main color from beanie, sew beard panel onto hat as shown below. Fasten off. Weave in ends.

With hat turned wrong side out, align the beard panel diagonally with the lower edge of the beanie. One end should be on the last row, and one should be three rows above.

Luvbug Slouchy

Snuggle your noggin in this super cute and soft hat. My young twins enjoy wearing it because of the fun texture.

Skill Level

Intermediate

Finished Measurements

Head circumference: Small: 15–17.5"/34–44.5 cm, Medium: 17.5–19"/44.5–48 cm, Large: 19–22.5"/48–57 cm

Yarn

- Red Heart Soft Yarn, medium worsted weight #4 yarn (100% acrylic; 256 yd/5 oz, 234 m/142 g per skein)
    1 skein #4601 Off White (Color A)
- Sensations Lovebug, bulky weight #5 yarn (100% polyester; 102 yd/3.5 oz, 93 m/100 g per skein)
    1 skein #49905 Light Green (Color B)

Hook and Other Materials

- F-5 (3.75 mm) hook or size to obtain gauge
- Stitch marker (optional)

Gauge

14 sts and 20 rows in sc = 4"/10 cm square

Notes

1. The hat is worked from the bottom up in continuous rounds. If you like, you can use a stitch marker to mark the first stitch of each round for reference.
2. Work loosely with the Lovebug yarn (Color B). You can pull some bobbles through and make other stitches tighter to vary the texture of the yarn.
3. When you change colors, you will carry the old yarn, instead of fastening it off. That will allow you to simply pick the yarn up later, with no ends to weave in. For a tutorial, see page 132.
4. To change colors, push the hook through the last stitch of the first color, pull the yarn back through, yarn over with the NEXT color, and pull through. Color change is complete. Also see page 131 for a tutorial.
5. This hat is very easy to customize—make the stripes wider, add extra stripes, or mix up multiple stripe colors. You'll see in the photos I added an extra stripe of the Lovebug Yarn to the larger hat.
6. See page 129 for a tutorial on Front Post Double Crochet (fpdc), page 130 for Back Post Double Crochet (bpdc), page 124 for crocheting through the Back Loop Only (blo), page 126 for Single Crochet Decrease (sc dec), and page 134 for how to make a pom-pom.

Hat

SMALL

Using Color A, ch48, sl st to first chain to join.
Rounds 1–5: Ch2, * bpdc, fpdc2, repeat from * to complete round, sl st to first stitch to join (48 sts).
Round 6: Ch1, sc in each stitch.
Round 7: Working continuously in the round, sc in each stitch.
Round 8: Drop Color A, join Color B, loosely sc in each stitch.
Round 9: Drop Color B, pick up Color A, sc in blo of each stitch.
Rounds 10–11: Sc in each stitch.
Round 12: Drop Color A, pick up Color B, loosely sc in each stitch.
Round 13: Repeat Round 9.
Rounds 14–15: Repeat Round 10.
Round 16: Repeat Round 12.
Round 17: Repeat Round 9.
Rounds 18–19: Repeat Round 10.
Round 20: Repeat Round 12.
Round 21: Drop Color B, pick up Color A, * sc6, sc dec, repeat from * to complete round (42 sts).
Round 22: * Sc5, sc dec, repeat from * to complete round (36 sts).

Round 23: * Sc4, sc dec, repeat from * to complete round (30 sts).
Round 24: * Sc3, sc dec, repeat from * to complete round (24 sts).
Round 25: * Sc2, sc dec, repeat from * to complete round (18 sts).
Round 26: * Sc, sc dec, repeat from * to complete round (12 sts).
Round 27: Sc dec 6 times, sl st to first stitch to join (6 sts).
Round 28: Sc in each stitch, sl st to first stitch to join. Fasten off, leaving a long tail to close top.

MEDIUM

Using Color A, ch54, sl st to first chain to join.
Rounds 1–5: Ch2, * bpdc, fpdc2, repeat from * to complete round, sl st to first stitch to join (54 sts).
Round 6: Ch1, sc in each stitch.
Rounds 7–8: Working continuously in the round, sc in each stitch.
Round 9: Drop Color A, join Color B, loosely sc in each stitch.
Round 10: Drop Color B, pick up Color A, sc in blo of each stitch.

Rounds 11–13: Sc in each stitch.
Round 14: Drop Color A, pick up Color B, loosely sc in each stitch.
Round 15: Repeat Round 10.
Rounds 16–18: Repeat Round 11.
Round 19: Repeat Round 14.
Round 20: Repeat Round 10.
Rounds 21–23: Repeat Round 11.
Round 24: Repeat Round 14.
Round 25: Drop Color B, pick up Color A, * sc7, sc dec, repeat from * to complete round (48 sts).
Round 26: * Sc6, sc dec, repeat from * to complete round (42 sts).
Round 27: * Sc5, sc dec, repeat from * to complete round (36 sts).
Round 28: * Sc4, sc dec, repeat from * to complete round (30 sts).
Round 29: * Sc3, sc dec, repeat from * to complete round (24 sts).
Round 30: * Sc2, sc dec, repeat from * to complete round (18 sts).
Round 31: * Sc, sc dec, repeat from * to complete round (12 sts).

Round 32: Sc dec 6 times, sl st to first stitch to join (6 sts).

Round 33: Sc in each stitch, sl st to first stitch to join.
Fasten off, leaving a long tail to close top.

LARGE

Using Color A, ch70, sl st to first chain to join.

Rounds 1–5: Ch2, * bpdc, fpdc2, repeat from * to complete round, sl st to first stitch to join (70 sts).

Round 6: Ch1, sc in each stitch.

Rounds 7–9: Working continuously in the round, sc in each stitch.

Round 10: Drop Color A, join Color B, loosely sc in each stitch.

Round 11: Drop Color B, pick up Color A, sc in blo of each stitch.

Rounds 12–15: Sc in each stitch.

Round 16: Drop Color A, pick up Color B, loosely sc in each stitch.

Round 17: Repeat Round 11.

Rounds 18–21: Repeat Round 12.

Round 22: Repeat Round 16.

Round 23: Repeat Round 11.

Rounds 24–27: Repeat Round 12.

Round 28: Repeat Round 16.

Round 29: Repeat Round 11.

Rounds 30–33: Repeat Round 12.

Round 34: Repeat Round 16.

Round 35: Drop Color B, pick up Color A, * sc5, sc dec, repeat from * to complete round (60 sts).

Round 36: * Sc4, sc dec, repeat from * to complete round (50 sts).

Round 37: * Sc3, sc dec, repeat from * to complete round (40 sts).

Round 38: * Sc2, sc dec, repeat from * to complete round (30 sts).

Round 39: * Sc, sc dec, repeat from * to complete round (20 sts).

Round 40: Sc dec 10 times, sl st to first stitch to join (10 sts).

Round 41: Sc in each stitch, sl st to first stitch to join.
Fasten off, leaving a long tail to close top.

Finishing

Using crochet hook, weave long tail through stitches of last round, pull tight, and secure to finish.

Make 1 pom-pom in Color A and attach to top of hat.

Sweetheart Sunhat

This hat is perfect for tea time or picnics at the park! Make one for you, your girl, and grandma!

Skill Level
Beginner

Finished Measurements
Head circumference: Small: 15–17.5"/38–44.5 cm,
Medium: 17.5–19"/44.5–48 cm, Large: 19–22.5"/48–57 cm

Yarn
- Red Heart Soft Yarn, medium worsted weight #4 yarn
  (100% acrylic; 204 yd/4 oz, 187 m/113 g per skein)
     1 skein #4420 Guacamole (Color A)
     1 skein #9114 Honey (Color B)
- Lion Brand Vanna's Choice, medium worsted weight #4
  yarn (100% acrylic; 170 yd/3.5 oz, 155 m/100 g per skein)
     1 skein #860-143 Antique Rose (Color C)

Hook and Other Materials
- H-8 (5.0 mm) hook or size to obtain gauge
- 2 medium buttons
- Sewing needle and thread
- Stitch marker (optional)

Gauge
Using Color A, 14 sts and 16 rows in sc = 4"/10 cm square

Notes
1. The hat is worked from the top down in continuous
   rounds. If you like, you can place a stitch marker at the
   beginning of each round for reference.
2. The flower is made in one piece, and then slipped over
   the button to finish.

Hat

SMALL
Using Color A, ch4, sl st to first chain to create a ring.
Round 1: Ch1, 10sc in ring (10 sts).
Round 2: Working continuously in the round, 2sc in each
stitch (20 sts).
Round 3: * Sc, 2sc in next stitch, repeat from * to complete
round (30 sts).
Round 4: * Sc2, 2sc in next stitch, repeat from * to complete
round (40 sts).
Round 5: * Sc3, 2sc in next stitch, repeat from * to complete
round (50 sts).
Rounds 6–16: Sc in each stitch.
Round 17: * Sc4, 2sc in next stitch, repeat from * to
complete round (60 sts).
Round 18: * Sc5, 2sc in next stitch, repeat from * to
complete round (70 sts).
Round 19: * Sc6, 2sc in next stitch, repeat from * to
complete round (80 sts).
Round 20: * Sc7, 2sc in next stitch, repeat from * to
complete round (90 sts).
Round 21: * Sc8, 2sc in next stitch, repeat from * to
complete round (100 sts).
Round 22: * Sc9, 2sc in next stitch, repeat from * to
complete round (110 sts).
Round 23: Sc in each stitch.
Fasten off. Weave in ends.

MEDIUM
Using Color A, ch4, sl st to first chain to create a ring.
Round 1: Ch1, 10sc in ring (10 sts).
Round 2: Working continuously in the round, 2sc in each
stitch (20 sts).
Round 3: * Sc, 2sc in next stitch, repeat from * to complete
round (30 sts).
Round 4: * Sc2, 2sc in next stitch, repeat from * to complete
round (40 sts).
Round 5: * Sc3, 2sc in next stitch, repeat from * to complete
round (50 sts).
Round 6: * Sc4, 2sc in next stitch, repeat from * to complete
round (60 sts).
Rounds 7–19: Sc in each stitch.
Round 20: * Sc5, 2sc in next stitch, repeat from * to
complete round (70 sts).
Round 21: * Sc6, 2sc in next stitch, repeat from * to
complete round (80 sts).

Round 22: * Sc7, 2sc in next stitch, repeat from * to complete round (90 sts).

Round 23: * Sc8, 2sc in next stitch, repeat from * to complete round (100 sts).

Round 24: * Sc9, 2sc in next stitch, repeat from * to complete round (110 sts).

Round 25: * Sc10, 2sc in next stitch, repeat from * to complete round (120 sts).

Round 26: Sc in each stitch.
Fasten off. Weave in ends.

LARGE

Using Color B, ch4, sl st to first chain to create a ring.

Round 1: Ch1, 10sc in ring (10 sts).

Round 2: Working continuously in the round, 2sc in each stitch (20 sts).

Round 3: * Sc, 2sc in next stitch, repeat from * to complete round (30 sts).

Round 4: * Sc2, 2sc in next stitch, repeat from * to complete round (40 sts).

Round 5: * Sc3, 2sc in next stitch, repeat from * to complete round (50 sts).

Round 6: * Sc4, 2sc in next stitch, repeat from * to complete round (60 sts).
Round 7: * Sc5, 2sc in next stitch, repeat from * to complete round (70 sts).
Rounds 8–23: Sc in each stitch.
Round 24: * Sc6, 2sc in next stitch, repeat from * to complete round (80 sts).
Round 25: * Sc7, 2sc in next stitch, repeat from * to complete round (90 sts).
Round 26: * Sc8, 2sc in next stitch, repeat from * to complete round (100 sts).
Round 27: * Sc9, 2sc in next stitch, repeat from * to complete round (110 sts).
Round 28: * Sc10, 2sc in next stitch, repeat from * to complete round (120 sts).
Round 29: * Sc11, 2sc in next stitch, repeat from * to complete round (130 sts).
Round 30: * Sc12, 2sc in next stitch, repeat from * to complete round (140 sts).
Round 31: * Sc13, 2sc in next stitch, repeat from * to complete round (150 sts).
Round 32: Sc in each stitch.
Fasten off. Weave in ends.

Flower

Using Color C, ch5, sl st to first chain to join.
Round 1: Ch1, 6sc in ring, sl st to first stitch to join (6 sts).
Round 2: Ch1, * (sl st, ch1, dc, ch1, sl st) in next stitch, repeat from * to complete round, sl st to first sl st to join (6 petals).
Round 3: Ch4, sl st to space between first two petals, * ch3, sl st to space between next two petals, repeat from * to complete round (6 ch3 spaces).
Round 4: Ch1, (sl st, ch1, 3dc, ch1, sl st) in each ch3 space, sl st to beginning ch1 to join round (6 petals).
Round 5: Repeat Round 3.
Round 6: Repeat Round 4.
Fasten off. Weave in ends.

Finishing

Flip front side of brim up and sew button on through both layers to hold in place.

Adjust flower layers if needed so that smaller petals are in front and slip over button to finish.

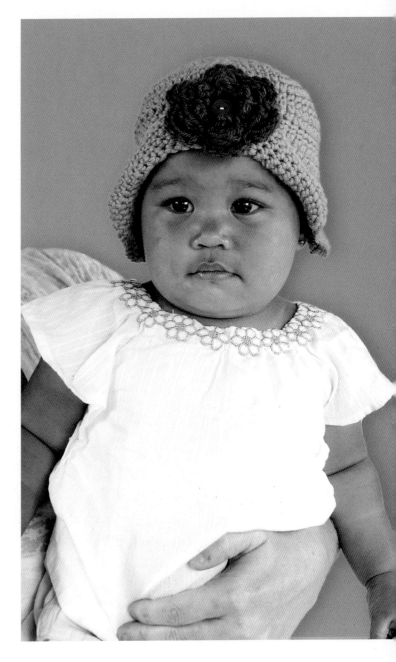

Lamb Bonnet

Momma had a sweet little lamb … the yarn was soft as snow. And everywhere that Momma went, her crochet bag was in tow!

Skill Level
Beginner

Finished Measurements
Head circumference: Small: 15–17.5"/38–44.5 cm, Medium: 17.5–19"/44.5–48 cm, Large: 19–22.5"/48–57 cm

Yarn
- Deborah Norville Serenity Chunky, bulky weight #5 yarn (100% fine acrylic; 109 yd/3.5 oz, 100 m/100 g per skein)
    1 skein #7036 Fudge (Color A)
    1 skein #7021 Pristine (Color B)
- Lion Brand Vanna's Choice, medium worsted weight #4 yarn (100% acrylic; 170 yd/3.5 oz, 155 m/100 g per skein)
    1 skein #860-101 Pink (Color C)

Hook and Other Materials
- N-13 (9.0 mm) hook or size to obtain gauge
- H-8 (5.0 mm) hook or size to obtain gauge
- Yarn needle

Gauge
Using N-13 (9.0 mm) hook and Color A or B, 12 sts and 5 rows in dc = 4"/10 cm square
Using H-8 (5.0 mm) hook and Color C, 16 sts and 7 rows in dc = 4"/10 cm square

Notes
1. The bonnet is worked in a panel, and sewn up in the back to finish.
2. The ch3 at the beginning of each row counts as the first stitch.
3. See page 128 for a tutorial on Double Crochet Decrease (dc dec).

Special Technique
Cluster

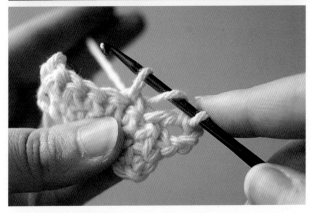

1 Yarn over, insert hook into stitch, yarn over, and pull yarn back through: 3 loops on hook.

2 Yarn over, pull yarn through first 2 loops: 2 loops on hook.

(continued)

3 Yarn over, insert hook into SAME stitch, yarn over, and pull yarn back through: 4 loops on hook.

4 Yarn over, pull yarn through first 2 loops: 3 loops on hook.

5 Yarn over, pull yarn through all loops. Cluster is complete.

Hat

SMALL

Using N-13 (9.0 mm) hook and Color A, ch 25.
Row 1: Turn, sc in second chain from hook and in each chain across (24 sts).
Rows 2–8: Turn, ch3, Cluster in each stitch.
Row 9: Turn, ch3, Cluster8, dc dec 4 times, Cluster8 (20 sts).
Fasten off, leaving a long tail to sew back together.

MEDIUM

Using N-13 (9.0 mm) hook and Color A, ch29.
Row 1: Turn, sc in second chain from hook and in each chain acorss (28 sts).
Rows 2–9: Turn, ch3, Cluster in each stitch.
Row 10: Turn, ch3, Cluster10, dc dec 4 times, Cluster10 (24 sts).
Fasten off, leaving a long tail to sew back together.

LARGE

Using N-13 (9.0 mm) hook and Color B, ch35.
Row 1: Turn, sc in second chain from hook and in each chain across (34 sts).
Rows 2–11: Turn, ch3, Cluster in each stitch.
Row 12: Turn, ch3, Cluster13, dc dec 4 times, Cluster13 (30 sts).
Fasten off, leaving a long tail to sew back together.

Ears

OUTSIDE (MAKE 2)

Using N-13 (9.0 mm) hook and Color A or B, ch 15.
Round 1: Turn, dc in third chain from hook, dc 11, dc6 in last stitch; working on opposite side of chain, dc12 (30 sts). Fasten off.
Round 2: Join Color A or B at stitch 1 from Round 1, ch1, sl st 15, (sl st, ch3, sl st) in next stitch, sl st 14. Fasten off, leaving a long tail to sew onto hat.

INSIDE (MAKE 2)

Using H-8 (5.0 mm) hook and Color C, ch 15.
Round 1: Turn, dc in third chain from hook, dc 11, dc6 in last stitch; working on opposite side of chain, dc12 (30 sts). Fasten off, leaving a long tail to sew onto Back.

Ties (make 2)

For each tie: Cut 2 lengths of Color A or B 3'/1 m long. Align the ends, then, holding them together, fold in half. With a crochet hook, pull the center fold through the stitch in one of the bottom front corners of the hat. Take hold of the cut ends and thread them through the fold. Pull tight on the ends.

Finishing

Using yarn needle, sew last row of panel together with running stitch.

With yarn needle, sew outer and inner ears together. Sew bottom corners of ear together to create shape. Sew completed ears onto either side of bonnet. Fasten off. Weave in ends.

Just Like Mommy
Ribbed Beanie

Like mother, like daughter. This sweet set is perfect for outings in cool weather. Mix and match the flowers and stripes and you'll be the most darling "Mommy and Me" in town!

Skill Level

Intermediate

Finished Measurements

Head circumference: X-Small: 12–14.5"/30.5–37 cm, Small: 15–17.5"/38–44.5 cm, Medium: 17.5–19"/44.5–48 cm, Large: 19–22.5"/48–57 cm
Height: X-Small: 4.5–6"/11.5–15 cm, Small: 6–6.5"/15–16.5 cm, Medium: 6.5–7"/16.5–18 cm, Large: 7–7.5"/18–19 cm

Yarn

- I Love This Cotton!, medium worsted weight #4 yarn (100% cotton; 180 yd/3.5 oz, 165 m/100 g per skein)
    1 skein #48 Taupe (Color A)
    1 skein #20 Brown (Color B)
    1 skein #254 Rosy (Color C)

Hook and Other Materials

- 7 (4.75 mm) hook or size needed to obtain gauge
- Yarn needle

Gauge

12 sts and 8 rows in dc = 4"/10 cm square

Notes

1. The beanie is worked from the top down.
2. The flower is made separately and then sewn onto the beanie.
3. The ch2 at the beginning of each round does not count as a stitch.
4. When changing colors, you will carry the old yarn, instead of fastening it off. That will allow you to simply pick the yarn up later, with no ends to weave in. For a tutorial, see page 132.
5. To change colors, push the hook through the last stitch of the first color, pull the yarn back through, yarn over with the NEXT color, and pull through. Color change is complete. Also see page 131 for a tutorial.
6. See page 129 for a tutorial on Front Post Double Crochet (fpdc) and page 126 for Single Crochet Decrease (sc dec).

Hat

X-SMALL

Using Color A, ch4.
Round 1: 10dc in fourth chain from hook, sl st to first stitch to join round (10 sts).
Round 2: Ch2, (fpdc, dc) in each stitch, sl st to first stitch to join (20 sts).
Round 3: Ch2, * 2dc in next stitch, fpdc, repeat from * to complete round, sl st to first stitch to join (30 sts).
Round 4: Ch2, * 2dc in next stitch, dc, fpdc, repeat from * to complete round, sl st to first stitch to join (40 sts).
Rounds 5–9: Ch2, * dc3, fpdc, repeat from * to complete round, sl st to first stitch to join.
Rounds 10–11: Ch1, sc in each stitch, sl st to first stitch to join.
Round 12: Join Color B, drop Color A, ch1, sc in each stitch, sl st to first st to join.
Round 13: Drop Color B, pick up Color A, ch1, sc in each stitch, sl st to first st to join.
Round 14: Drop Color A, pick up Color B, ch1, sc in each stitch, sl st to first st to join.
Round 15: Repeat Round 13.
Fasten off. Weave in ends.

SMALL

Using Color A, ch4.

Round 1: 8dc in fourth chain from hook, sl st to first stitch to join round (8 sts).

Round 2: Ch2, (fpdc, dc) in each stitch, sl st to first stitch to join (16 sts).

Round 3: Ch2, * 2dc in next stitch, fpdc, repeat from * to complete round, sl st to first stitch to join (24 sts).

Round 4: Ch2, * 2dc in next stitch, dc, fpdc, repeat from * to complete round, sl st to first stitch to join (32 sts).

Round 5: Ch2, * 2dc in next stitch, dc2, fpdc, repeat from * to complete round, sl st to first stitch to join (40 sts).

Round 6: Ch2, * 2dc in next stitch, dc3, fpdc, repeat from * to complete round, sl st to first stitch to join (48 sts).

Rounds 7–11: Ch2, dc in each stitch, sl st to first stitch to join.

Rounds 12–13: Ch1, sc in each stitch.

Round 14: Join Color B, drop Color A, ch1, sc in each stitch, sl st to first st to join.

Round 15: Drop Color B, pick up Color A, ch1, sc in each stitch, sl st to first st to join.

Round 16: Drop Color A, pick up Color B, ch1, sc in each stitch, sl st to first st to join.

Round 17: Repeat Round 15.

Round 18: Repeat Round 12.

Fasten off. Weave in ends.

MEDIUM

Using Color B, ch4.

Round 1: 11dc in fourth chain from hook, sl st to first stitch to join round (11 sts).

Round 2: Ch2, (fpdc, dc) in each stitch, sl st to first stitch to join (22 sts).

Round 3: Ch2, * 2dc in next stitch, fpdc, repeat from * to complete round, sl st to first stitch to join (33 sts).

Round 4: Ch2, * 2dc in next stitch, dc, fpdc, repeat from * to complete round, sl st to first stitch to join (44 sts).

Round 5: Ch2, * 2dc in next stitch, dc2, fpdc, repeat from * to complete round, sl st to first stitch to join (55 sts).

Rounds 6–14: Ch2, dc in each stitch, sl st to first stitch to join.

Round 15: Ch1, sc in each stitch, sl st to first stitch to join.

Round 16: Ch1, * sc 9, sc dec, repeat from * to complete round, sl st to first stitch to join (50 sts).

Round 17: Join Color C, drop Color B, ch1, sc in each stitch, sl st to first stitch to join.

Round 18: Drop Color C, pick up Color B, ch1, sc in each stitch, sl st to first stitch to join.

Rounds 19–20: Repeat Round 15.

Fasten off. Weave in ends.

LARGE

Using Color B, ch4.

Round 1: 10dc in fourth chain from hook, sl st to first stitch to join round (10 sts).

Round 2: Ch2, (fpdc, dc) in each stitch, sl st to first stitch to join round (20 sts).

Round 3: Ch2, * 2dc in next stitch, fpdc, repeat from * to complete round, sl st to first stitch to join (30 sts).

Round 4: Ch2, * 2dc in next stitch, dc, fpdc, repeat from * to complete round, sl st to first stitch to join (40 sts).

Round 5: Ch2, * 2dc in next stitch, dc2, fpdc, repeat from * to complete round, sl st to first stitch to join (50 sts).

Round 6: Ch2, * 2dc in next stitch, dc3, fpdc, repeat from * to complete round, sl st to first stitch to join (60 sts).

Rounds 7–15: Ch2, dc in each stitch, sl st to first stitch to join.

Round 16: Ch1, sc in each stitch, sl st to first stitch to join.

Round 17: Ch1, * sc 8, sc dec, repeat from * to complete round, sl st to first stitch to join (54 sts).

Round 18: Join Color C, drop Color B, ch1, sc in each stitch, sl st to first stitch to join.

Round 19: Drop Color C, pick up Color B, ch1, sc in each stitch, sl st to first stitch to join.

Rounds 20–21: Repeat Round 16.

Fasten off. Weave in ends.

Flower

Using Color C, ch26.

Row 1: Turn, dc in fourth chain from hook, * (dc, ch3, dc) in next chain, repeat from * in each chain.

Fasten off, leaving long tail to sew together.

Roll flower up; using yarn needle, sew together and onto hat. Fasten off. Weave in ends.

Basketweave Beanie

This classic beanie is a beauty to make in any color. The basketweave is stunning and is perfect for kids of all ages!

Skill Level

Advanced

Finished Measurements

Head circumference: Small: 15–17.5"/38–44.5 cm, Medium: 17.5–19"/44.5–48 cm, Large: 19–22.5"/48–57 cm
Height: Small: 6–6.5"/15–16.5 cm, Medium: 6.5–7"/16.5–18 cm, Large: 7–7.5"/18–19 cm

Yarn

• Lion Brand Pound of Love Yarn, medium worsted weight #4 yarn (100% acrylic; 1,020 yd/16.00 oz, 932 m/454 g per skein)
   1 skein #550-110 Denim

Hook and Other Materials

• F-5 (3.75 mm) hook or size to obtain gauge

Gauge

16 sts and 20 rows in dc = 4"/10 cm square

Notes

1. The hat is worked from the bottom up in rounds.
2. The ch2 at the beginning of each round does not count as a stitch.
3. See page 129 for a tutorial on Front Post Double Crochet (fpdc) and page 130 for Back Post Double Crochet (bpdc).

Basketweave pattern looks complicated, but is actually really simple to create. By alternating fpdc and bpdc in a specific pattern, you will create a beautiful texture that appears to "weave" in and out of the hat.

Special Technique
Front Post Double Crochet Decrease (fpdc dec)

1 Yarn over and insert hook around the post of the stitch from front to back to front.

2 Yarn over and pull yarn back around post: 3 loops on hook.

3 Yarn over and draw yarn through first 2 loops on hook: 2 loops on hook.

(continued)

4 Yarn over and insert hook around the post of the next stitch from front to back of front. Yarn over and pull yarn back around post: 4 loops on hook.

5 Yarn over and draw yarn through first 2 loops on hook: 3 loops on hook.

6 Yarn over and draw yarn through the remaining 3 loops on hook to complete the stitch.

Hat

SMALL

Ch65.

Round 1: Turn, sc in second chain from hook and in each chain across, sl st to first stitch to join (64 sts).

Rounds 2–4: Ch1, sc in each stitch.

Round 5: Ch2, * bpdc3, fpdc5, repeat from * to complete round, sl st to first stitch to join.

Rounds 6–7: Repeat Round 5.

Rounds 8–10: Ch2, fpdc3, bpdc5, repeat from * to complete round, sl st to first stitch to join.

Rounds 11–13: Repeat Round 5.

Rounds 14–16: Repeat Round 8.

Round 17: Ch2, * fpdc6, fpdc dec (see Special Technique), repeat from * to complete round, sl st to first stitch to join (56 sts).

Round 18: Ch2, * fpdc5, fpdc dec, repeat from * to complete round, sl st to first stitch to join (48 sts).

Round 19: Ch2, * fpdc4, fpdc dec, repeat from * to complete round, sl st to first stitch to join (40 sts).

Round 20: Ch2, * fpdc3, fpdc dec, repeat from * to complete round, sl st to first stitch to join (32 sts).

Round 21: Ch2, * fpdc2, fpdc dec, repeat from * to complete round, sl st to first stitch to join (24 sts).

Round 22: Ch2, * fpdc, fpdc dec, repeat from* to complete round, sl st to first stitch to join (16 sts).

Round 23: Ch2, fpdc dec 8 times, sl st to first stitch to join (8 sts).

Round 24: Ch2, fpdc in each stitch, sl st to first stitch to join. Fasten off.

Finish top by weaving end in and out of last 8 stitches; pull tight. Fasten off. Weave in ends.

MEDIUM

Ch73.

Round 1: Turn, sc in second chain from hook and in each chain across, sl st to first stitch to join (72 sts).

Rounds 2–4: Ch1, sc in each stitch.

Round 5: Ch2, * bpdc3, fpdc5, repeat from * to complete round, sl st to first stitch to join.

Rounds 6–7: Repeat Round 5.

Rounds 8–10: Ch2, fpdc3, bpdc5, repeat from * to complete round, sl st to first stitch to join.

Rounds 11–13: Repeat Round 5.

Rounds 14–16: Repeat Round 8.

Round 17: Ch2, * fpdc7, fpdc dec (see Special Technique), repeat from * to complete round, sl st to first stitch to join (64 sts).

Round 18: Ch2, * fpdc6, fpdc dec, repeat from * to complete round, sl st to first stitch to join (56 sts).

Round 19: Ch2, * fpdc5, fpdc dec, repeat from * to complete round, sl st to first stitch to join (48 sts).

Round 20: Ch2, * fpdc4, fpdc dec, repeat from * to complete round, sl st to first stitch to join (40 sts).
Round 21: Ch2, * fpdc3, fpdc dec, repeat from * to complete round, sl st to first stitch to join (32 sts).
Round 22: Ch2, * fpdc2, fpdc dec, repeat from * to complete round, sl st to first stitch to join (24 sts).
Round 23: Ch2, * fpdc, fpdc dec, repeat from * to complete round, sl st to first stitch to join (16 sts).
Round 24: Ch2, fpdc dec 8 times, sl st to first stitch to join (8 sts).
Round 25: Ch2, fpdc in each stitch, sl st to first stitch to join. Fasten off.
Finish top by weaving end in and out of last 8 stitches; pull tight. Fasten off. Weave in ends.

LARGE

Ch81.
Round 1: Turn, sc in second chain from hook and in each chain across, sl st to first stitch to join (80 sts).
Rounds 2–4: Ch1, sc in each stitch.
Round 5: Ch2, * bpdc3, fpdc5, repeat from * to complete round, sl st to first stitch to join.
Rounds 6–7: Repeat Round 5.
Rounds 8–10: Ch2, fpdc3, bpdc5, repeat from * to complete round, sl st to first stitch to join.
Rounds 11–13: Repeat Round 5.
Rounds 14–16: Repeat Round 8.
Rounds 17–19: Repeat Round 5.
Round 20: Ch2, * fpdc8, fpdc dec (see Special Technique), repeat from * to complete round, sl st to first stitch to join (72 sts).
Round 21: Ch2, * fpdc7, fpdc dec, repeat from * to complete round, sl st to first stitch to join (64 sts).
Round 22: Ch2, * fpdc6, fpdc dec, repeat from * to complete round, sl st to first stitch to join (56 sts).
Round 23: Ch2, * fpdc5, fpdc dec, repeat from * to complete round, sl st to first stitch to join (48 sts).
Round 24: Ch2, * fpdc4, fpdc dec, repeat from * to complete round, sl st to first stitch to join (40 sts).
Round 25: Ch2, * fpdc3, fpdc dec, repeat from * to complete round, sl st to first stitch to join (32 sts).
Round 26: Ch2, * fpdc2, fpdc dec, repeat from * to complete round, sl st to first stitch to join (24 sts).
Round 27: Ch2, * fpdc, fpdc dec, repeat from * to complete round, sl st to first stitch to join (16 sts).
Round 28: Ch2, fpdc dec 8 times, sl st to first stitch to join (8 sts).
Round 29: Ch2, fpdc in each stitch, sl st to first stitch to join. Fasten off.
Finish top by weaving end in and out of last 8 stitches; pull tight. Fasten off. Weave in ends.

Buddy
Bobbles

Turn something plain into something fantastic with color and bobbles! This hat is a blast to crochet AND wear!

Skill Level

Beginner

Finished Measurements

Head circumference: X-Small: 12–14.5"/30.5–37 cm, Small: 15–17.5"/38–44.5 cm, Medium: 17.5–19"/44.5–48 cm, Large: 19–22.5"/48–57 cm, X-Large: 23–24.5"/58.5–62 cm
Height: X-Small: 4.5–6"/11.5–15 cm, Small: 6–6.5"/15–16.5 cm, Medium: 6.5–7"/16.5–18 cm, Large: 7–7.5"/18–19 cm, X-Large: 7.5–8"/19–20.5– cm

Yarn

- Lion Brand Jiffy Yarn, bulky weight #5 yarn (100% acrylic; 135 yd/3 oz, 123 m/85 g per skein)
    - 1 skein #450-155 Silver Heather (Color A)
    - 1 skein #450-132 Apple Green (Color B)
    - 1 skein #450-171 Aqua (Color C)

Hook and Other Materials

- H-8 (5.0 mm) hook or size to obtain gauge

Gauge

10 sts and 13 rows in sc = 4"/10 cm square

Notes

1. The beanie is worked from the top down in rounds.
2. The ch1 at the beginning of rounds does not count as a stitch.
3. When changing colors, you will carry the old yarn, instead of fastening it off. That will allow you to simply pick the yarn up later, with no ends to weave in. For a tutorial, see page 132.
4. To change colors, push the hook through the last stitch of the first color, pull the yarn back through, then yarn over with the NEXT color, and pull through. Color change is complete. Also see page 131 for a tutorial.
5. See page 126 for a tutorial on Single Crochet Decrease (sc dec).

Special Technique
Bobble Stitch

1 Yarn over and insert hook into stitch. Yarn over and pull yarn back through stitch: 3 loops on hook.

2 Yarn over and draw yarn through first 2 loops on hook: 2 loops on hook.

3 Yarn over and insert hook into same stitch. Yarn over and pull yarn back through stitch: 4 loops on hook.

4 Yarn over and draw yarn through first 2 loops on hook: 3 loops on hook.

5 Yarn over and insert hook into same stitch. Yarn over and pull yarn back through stitch: 5 loops on hook.

6 Yarn over and draw yarn through first 2 loops on hook: 4 loops on hook.

7 Yarn over and insert hook into same stitch. Yarn over and pull yarn back through stitch: 6 loops on hook.

8 Yarn over and draw yarn through first 2 loops on hook: 5 loops on hook.

9 Yarn over and draw yarn through all 5 loops on hook to complete.

Hat

X-SMALL

Using Color A, ch4, sl st to first chain to create a ring.
Round 1: Ch1, 10sc in ring, sl st to first stitch to join (10 sts).
Round 2: 2sc in each stitch, sl st to first stitch to join (20 sts).
Round 3: * Sc, 2sc in next stitch, repeat from * to complete round, sl st to first stitch to join (30 sts).
Round 4: * Sc2, 2sc in next stitch, repeat from * to complete round, sl st to first stitch to join (40 sts).
Round 5: Drop Color A, join Color B, * sc3, Bobble (see Special Technique), repeat from * to complete round, sl st to first stitch to join.
Round 6: Drop Color B, pick up Color A, ch1, sc in each stitch, sl st to first stitch to join.
Round 7: Ch1, sc in each stitch, sl st to first stitch to join.
Round 8: Drop Color A, pick up Color B, sc, Bobble, *sc3, Bobble, repeat from * to last 2 sts, sc2, sl st to first stitch to join.
Rounds 9–10: Repeat Rounds 6–7.
Round 11: Drop Color A, pick up Color B, * sc3, Bobble, repeat from * to complete round, sl st to first stitch to join.
Rounds 12–13: Repeat Rounds 6–7.
Round 14: Repeat Round 8.
Round 15: Repeat Round 6.
Rounds 16–17: Repeat Round 7.
Fasten off. Weave in ends.

SMALL

Using Color A, ch4, sl st to first chain to create a ring.
Round 1: Ch1, 10sc in ring, sl st to first stitch to join (10 sts).
Round 2: Ch1, 2sc in each stitch, sl st to first stitch to join (20 sts).
Round 3: Ch1, * sc, 2sc in next stitch, repeat from * to complete round, sl st to first stitch to join (30 sts).
Round 4: Ch1, * sc2, 2sc in next stitch, repeat from * to complete round, sl st to first stitch to join (40 sts).
Round 5: Ch1, * sc3, 2sc in next stitch, repeat from * to complete round, sl st to first stitch to join (50 sts).
Round 6: Drop Color A, join Color B, * sc4, Bobble (see Special Technique), repeat from * to complete round, sl st to first stitch to join.
Round 7: Drop Color B, pick up Color A, ch1, sc in each stitch, sl st to first stitch to join.
Round 8: Ch1, sc in each stitch, sl st to first stitch to join.
Round 9: Drop Color A, pick up Color B, sc, Bobble, *sc4, Bobble, repeat from * to last 3 sts, sc3, sl st to first stitch to join.
Rounds 10–11: Repeat Rounds 7–8.
Round 12: Drop Color A, pick up Color B, * sc4, Bobble, repeat from * to complete round, sl st to first stitch to join.
Rounds 13–14: Repeat Rounds 7–8.
Round 15: Repeat Round 9.

Rounds 16–17: Repeat Rounds 7–8.
Round 18: Repeat Round 12.
Round 19: Repeat Round 7.
Rounds 20–22: Repeat Round 8.
Fasten off. Weave in ends.

MEDIUM

Using Color A, ch4, sl st to first chain to create a ring.
Round 1: Ch1, 10sc in ring, sl st to first stitch to join (10 sts).
Round 2: Ch1, 2sc in each stitch, sl st to first stitch to join (20 sts).
Round 3: Ch1, * sc, 2sc in next stitch, repeat from * to complete round, sl st to first stitch to join (30 sts).
Round 4: Ch1, * sc2, 2sc in next stitch, repeat from * to complete round, sl st to first stitch to join (40 sts).

Round 5: Ch1, * sc3, 2sc in next stitch, repeat from * to complete round, sl st to first stitch to join (50 sts).

Round 6: Ch1, * sc4, 2sc in next stitch, repeat from * to complete round, sl st to first stitch to join (60 sts).

Round 7: Drop Color A, join Color B, * sc4, Bobble (see Special Technique), repeat from * to complete round, sl st to first stitch to join.

Round 8: Drop Color B, pick up Color A, ch1, sc in each stitch, sl st to first stitch to join.

Round 9: Ch1, sc in each stitch, sl st to first stitch to join.

Round 10: Drop Color A, pick up Color B, sc, Bobble, *sc4, Bobble, repeat from * to last 3 sts, sc3, sl st to first stitch to join.

Rounds 11–12: Repeat Rounds 8–9.

Round 13: Drop Color A, pick up Color B, * sc4, Bobble, repeat from * to complete round, sl st to first stitch to join.

Rounds 14–15: Repeat Rounds 8–9.

Round 16: Repeat Round 10.

Rounds 17–18: Repeat Rounds 8–9.

Round 19: Repeat Round 13.

Round 20: Repeat Round 8.

Rounds 21–23: Repeat Round 9.

Fasten off. Weave in ends.

LARGE

Using Color A, ch4, sl st to first chain to create a ring.

Round 1: Ch1, 11sc in ring, sl st to first stitch to join (11 sts).

Round 2: Ch1, 2sc in each stitch, sl st to first stitch to join (22 sts).

Round 3: Ch1 * sc, 2sc in next stitch, repeat from * to complete round, sl st to first stitch to join (33 sts).

Round 4: Ch1, * sc2, 2sc in next stitch, repeat from * to complete round, sl st to first stitch to join (44 sts).

Round 5: Ch1, * sc3, 2sc in next stitch, repeat from * to complete round, sl st to first stitch to join (55 sts).

Round 6: Ch1, * sc4, 2sc in next stitch, repeat from * to complete round, sl st to first stitch to join (66 sts).

Rounds 7–8: Ch1, sc in each stitch, sl st to first stitch to join.

Round 9: Drop Color A, join Color C, * sc5, Bobble (see Special Technique), repeat from * to complete round, sl st to first stitch to join.

Round 10: Drop Color C, pick up Color A, ch1, sc in each stitch, sl st to first stitch to join.

Round 11: Repeat Round 7.

Round 12: Drop Color A, join Color B, sc2, Bobble, * sc5, Bobble, repeat from * to last 3 stitches, sc3, sl st to first stitch to join.

Rounds 13–14: Repeat Rounds 10–11.

Round 15: Drop Color A, pick up Color C, * sc5, Bobble, repeat from * to complete round, sl st to first stitch to join.

Rounds 16–17: Repeat Rounds 10–11.

Round 18: Repeat Round 12.

Rounds 19–20: Repeat Rounds 10–11.

Round 21: Repeat Round 15.

Rounds 22–23: Repeat Rounds 10–11.

Round 24: Ch1, * sc9, sc dec, repeat from * to complete round, sl st to first stitch to join (60 sts).

Rounds 25–26: Repeat Round 7.

Fasten off. Weave in ends.

X-LARGE

Using Color A, ch4, sl st to first chain to create a ring.

Round 1: Ch1, 12sc in ring, sl st to first stitch to join (12 sts).

Round 2: Ch1, 2sc in each stitch, sl st to first stitch to join (24 sts).

Round 3: Ch1 * sc, 2sc in next stitch, repeat from * to complete round, sl st to first stitch to join (36 sts).

Round 4: Ch1, * sc2, 2sc in next stitch, repeat from * to complete round, sl st to first stitch to join (48 sts).

Round 5: Ch1, * sc3, 2sc in next stitch, repeat from * to complete round, sl st to first stitch to join (60 sts).

Round 6: Ch1, * sc4, 2sc in next stitch, repeat from * to complete round, sl st to first stitch to join (72 sts).

Rounds 7–8: Ch1, sc in each stitch, sl st to first stitch to join.

Round 9: Drop Color A, join Color C, * sc5, Bobble (see Special Technique), repeat from * to complete round, sl st to first stitch to join.

Round 10: Drop Color C, pick up Color A, ch1, sc in each stitch, sl st to first stitch to join.

Round 11: Repeat Round 7.

Round 12: Drop Color A, join Color B, sc2, Bobble, * sc5, Bobble, repeat from * to last 3 stitches, sc3, sl st to first stitch to join.

Rounds 13–14: Repeat Rounds 10–11.

Round 15: Drop Color A, pick up Color C, * sc5, Bobble, repeat from * to complete round, sl st to first stitch to join.

Rounds 16–17: Repeat Rounds 10–11.

Round 18: Repeat Round 12.

Rounds 19–20: Repeat Rounds 10–11.

Round 21: Repeat Round 15.

Rounds 22–23: Repeat Rounds 10–11.

Round 24: Ch1, * sc4, sc dec, repeat from * to complete round, sl st to first stitch to join (60 sts).

Round 25–26: Repeat Round 7.

Fasten off. Weave in ends.

Winter Lodge Hat

$\mathcal{S}$tay warm and cozy in this snuggly hat. It reminds me of a snow trip in the mountains, spending time with family…just some Mommy, Daddy, and Me time!

Skill Level
Beginner

Finished Measurements
Head circumference: Small: 15–17.5"/38–44.5 cm, Medium: 17.5–19"/44.5–48 cm, Large: 19–22.5"/48–57 cm, X-Large: 23–24.5"/58.5–62 cm
Height: Small: 6–6.5"/15–16.5 cm, Medium: 6.5–7"/16.5–18 cm, Large: 7–7.5"/18–19 cm, X-Large: 7.5–8"/19–20.5 cm

Yarn
- Lion Brand Wool Ease Thick and Quick, super bulky weight #6 yarn (80% acrylic/20% wool; 106 yd/6 oz, 97 m/170 g per skein)
    1 skein #149 Charcoal (Color A)
    1 skein #640-105 Glacier (Color B)
- Lion Brand Homespun Thick and Quick, super bulky weight #6 yarn (88% acrylic/12% polyester; 160 yd/8 oz, 146 m/227 g per skein)
    1 skein #437 Dove (Color C)

Hook and Other Materials
- N-13 (9.0 mm) hook or size needed to obtain gauge
- 2 large buttons in coordinating color
- Sewing needle and thread
- Stitch marker (optional)

Gauge
6 sts and 9 rows in sc = 4"/10 cm square

Notes
1. The hat is worked from the top down continuously in the round. If you like, you can use a stitch marker to mark the first stitch of each round for reference.
2. The ch1 or ch2 at the beginning of the rounds and rows does not count as a stitch.
3. The foundation of the flap is crocheted right onto the hat.
4. See page 126 for a tutorial on Single Crochet Decrease (sc dec).

Special Technique
Cluster

1 Yarn over, insert hook into stitch, yarn over, and pull yarn back through: 3 loops on hook.

2 Yarn over, pull yarn through first 2 loops: 2 loops on hook.

(continued)

3 Yarn over, insert hook into SAME stitch, yarn over, and pull yarn back through: 4 loops on hook.

4 Yarn over, pull yarn through first 2 loops: 3 loops on hook.

5 Yarn over, pull yarn through all loops to complete the stitch.

Hat

SMALL

Using Color A, ch4.

Round 1: 10dc in fourth chain from hook, sl st to first stitch to join round (10 sts).

Round 2: Ch2, 2dc in each stitch, sl st to first stitch to join (20 sts).

Round 3: Ch2, * Cluster (see Special Technique), 2dc in next stitch, repeat from * to complete round. Sl st to first stitch to join (30 sts).

Round 4: Ch2, Cluster in each stitch, sl st to first stitch to join.

Round 5: Ch1, sc in each stitch, sl st to first stitch to join.

Round 6: Ch2, Cluster in each stitch, sl st to first stitch to join.

Rounds 7–9: Ch1, sc in each stitch, sl st to first stitch to join. Fasten off. Weave in ends.

MEDIUM

Using Color A, ch4.

Round 1: 10dc in fourth chain from hook, sl st to first stitch to join round (10 sts).

Round 2: Ch2, 2dc in each stitch, sl st to first stitch to join (20 sts).

Round 3: Ch2, * Cluster (see Special Techniques), 2dc in next stitch, repeat from * to complete round. Sl st to first stitch to join (30 sts).

Round 4: Ch2, * Cluster2, 2dc in next stitch, repeat from * to complete round. Sl st to first stitch to join (40 sts).

Round 5: Ch2, Cluster in each stitch, sl st to first stitch to join.

Round 6: Ch1, sc in each stitch, sl st to first stitch to join.

Round 7: Ch2, Cluster in each stitch, sl st to first stitch to join.

Rounds 8–11: Ch1, sc in each stitch, sl st to first stitch to join.

Fasten off. Weave in ends.

LARGE

Using Color B, ch4.

Round 1: 10dc in fourth chain from hook, sl st to first stitch to join round (10 sts).

Round 2: Ch2, 2dc in each stitch, sl st to first stitch to join (20 sts).

Round 3: Ch2, * Cluster (see Special Techniques), 2dc in next stitch, repeat from * to complete round. Sl st to first stitch to join (30 sts).

Round 4: Ch2, * Cluster2, 2dc in next stitch, repeat from * to complete round. Sl st to first stitch to join (40 sts).

Round 5: Ch2, * Cluster3, 2dc in next stitch, repeat from * to complete round. Sl st to first stitch to join (50 sts).

Round 6: Ch1, sc in each stitch, sl st to first stitch to join.

Round 7: Ch2, Cluster in each stitch, sl st to first stitch to join.

Round 8: Ch1, * sc9, sc dec, repeat from * to complete round. Sl st to first stitch to join (50 sts).
Round 9: Ch2, Cluster in each stitch, sl st to first stitch to join.
Round 10: Ch1, * sc3, sc dec, repeat from * to complete round. Sl st to first stitch to join (40 sts).
Rounds 11–12: Ch1, sc in each stitch, sl st to the first stitch to join.
Fasten off. Weave in ends.

Flap

SMALL

Join Color C in any stitch on the last round.
Row 1: Ch1, sc10 (10 sts).
Rows 2–5: Turn, ch1, sc10.
Fasten off. Weave in ends.

MEDIUM

Join Color C in any stitch on the last round.
Row 1: Ch1, sc12 (12 sts).
Rows 2–7: Turn, ch1, sc12.
Fasten off. Weave in ends.

LARGE

Join Color C in any stitch on the last round.
Row 1: Ch1, sc15 (15 sts).
Rows 2–9: Turn, ch1, sc15.
Fasten off. Weave in ends.

Finishing

Using sewing needles and thread, sew buttons onto top corners of flap to secure it to the hat and finish.

Round 8: Ch1, * sc8, sc dec, repeat from * to complete round. Sl st to first stitch to join (45 sts).
Round 9: Ch2, Cluster in each stitch, sl st to first stitch to join.
Round 10: Ch1, * sc3, sc dec, repeat from * to complete round. Sl st to first stitch to join (36 sts).
Rounds 11–12: Ch1, sc in each stitch, sl st to first stitch to join.
Fasten off. Weave in ends.

X-LARGE

Using Color B, ch4.
Round 1: 11dc in fourth chain from hook, sl st to first stitch to join round (11 sts).
Round 2: Ch2, 2dc in each stitch, sl st to first stitch to join (22 sts).
Round 3: Ch2, * Cluster (see Special Techniques), 2dc in next stitch, repeat from * to complete round, sl st to first stitch to join (33 sts).
Round 4: Ch2, * Cluster2, 2dc in next stitch, repeat from * to complete round. Sl st to first stitch to join (44 sts).
Round 5: Ch2, * Cluster3, 2dc in next stitch, repeat from * to complete round. Sl st to first stitch to join (55 sts).
Round 6: Ch1, sc in each stitch, sl st to first stitch to join.
Round 7: Ch2, Cluster in each stitch, sl st to first stitch to join.

Hooded Scarf

Never look for that missing scarf again! With this hat, your scarf is attached and you and your sweetie can wear it on the go!

Skill Level
Intermediate

Finished Measurements
Head circumference: Small: 15–17.5"/38–44.5 cm, Medium: 17.5–19"/44.5–48 cm, Large: 19–22.5"/48–57 cm

Yarn
• Lion Brand Hometown USA Yarn, super bulky weight #6 yarn (100% acrylic; 81 yd/4 oz, 74 m/113 g per skein)
   2 skeins #135-301 Santa Fe Tweed

Hook and Other Materials
• N-13 (9.0 mm) hook or size to obtain gauge
• 2 medium buttons
• Sewing thread and needle

Gauge
8 sts and 5 rows in dc = 4"/10 cm square

Notes
1. The hat and scarf are worked as one piece. The shell edging is added last, and is optional.

Hat

SMALL
Ch38.
Row 1: Turn, dc in third chain from hook, dc in each chain across (36 sts).
Row 2: Turn, ch2, hdc in each stitch.
Row 3: Turn, ch3, dc in each stitch.
Row 4: Turn, ch2, hdc in each stitch.
Row 5: Turn, ch3, dc30 (30 sts).
Row 6: Turn, ch2, hdc in each stitch.
Rows 7–12: Repeat Rows 5–6 three times.
Fasten off, leaving a long tail.
   Using yarn needle and tail, sew top together.

MEDIUM
Ch46.
Row 1: Turn, dc in third chain from hook, dc in each chain across (44 sts).
Row 2: Turn, ch2, hdc in each stitch.
Row 3: Turn, ch3, dc in each stitch.
Row 4: Turn, ch2, hdc in each stitch.
Row 5: Turn, ch3, dc34 (34 sts).
Row 6: Turn, ch2, hdc in each stitch.

The stitches on the scarf will easily slip over the buttons.

Rows 7–14: Repeat Rows 5–6 four times.
Fasten off, leaving a long tail.
   Using yarn needle and tail, sew top together.

LARGE

Ch56.
Row 1: Turn, dc in third chain from hook, dc in each chain across (54 sts).
Row 2: Turn, ch2, hdc in each stitch.
Row 3: Turn, ch3, dc in each stitch.
Row 4: Turn, ch2, hdc in each stitch.
Row 5: Turn, ch3, dc in each stitch.
Row 6: Turn, ch2, dc in each stitch.
Row 7: Turn, ch3, dc38 (38 sts).
Row 8: Turn, ch2, hdc in each stitch.
Rows 9–14: Repeat Rows 7–8 three times.
Fasten off, leaving a long tail.
   Using yarn needle and tail, sew top together.

Shell Edging

Join yarn at bottom corner of face opening opposite the scarf, ch3, 2dc in same stitch, skip 2 stitches, using ends of rows as stitches, sl st in next stitch, * skip 2 stitches, 5dc in next stitch, skip 2 stitches, sl st in next stitch, repeat from * to complete row, ending at top of scarf.

    Fasten off. Weave in ends.

Finishing

Using sewing needle and thread, sew two buttons on the edge opposite the scarf, then slip ch3 loops at the end of the scarf over buttons to finish.

Sassy Girl

Make your sassy girl the perfect sassy hat! Wear it for dressing up or going casual.

Skill Level

Beginner

Finished Measurements

Head circumference: Small: 15–17.5"/38–44.5 cm,
Medium: 17.5–19"/44.5–48 cm, Large: 19–22.5"/48–57 cm
Height: Small: 6–6.5"/15–16.5 cm, Medium: 6.5–7"/
16.5–18 cm, Large: 7–7.5"/18–19 cm

Yarn

- Red Heart Super Saver Yarn, medium worsted weight #4
  yarn (100% acrylic; 260 yd/5 oz, 238 m/142 g per skein)
    1 skein #4313 Aran Fleck (Color A)
    1 skein #0314 Black (Color B)

Hook and Other Materials

- H-8 (5.0 mm) hook or size to obtain gauge
- Yarn needle
- 5 small buttons
- Sewing needle and thread

Gauge

14 sts and 16 rows in sc = 4"/10 cm square

Notes

1. The hat is worked from the bottom up in rows. The top
   will be joined and worked in the round to finish.
2. The trim and buttons are added last.
3. When you change colors, you will carry the old yarn,
   instead of fastening it off. That will allow you to simply
   pick the yarn up later, with no ends to weave in. For a
   tutorial, see page 132.
4. To change colors, push the hook through the last stitch
   of the first color, pull the yarn back through, yarn over
   with the NEXT color, and pull through. Color change is
   complete. Also see page 131 for a tutorial.
5. See page 124 for a tutorial on crocheting into the Front
   Loop Only (flo) and Back Loop Only (blo).

Special Technique
Back Post Single Crochet (bpsc)

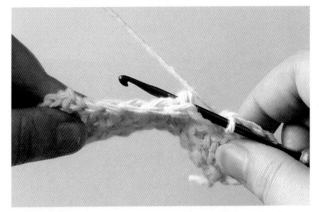

1 Insert hook around the post of the stitch from back to
  front to back.

2 Yarn over and pull yarn back around the post: 2 loops
  on hook

3 Yarn over and draw yarn through both loops on hook
  to complete.

Hat

SMALL

Using Color A, ch61.

Row 1: Turn, sc in second chain from hook and in each chain across (60 sts).

Row 2: Turn, ch2, hdc in each stitch.

Row 3: Turn, ch1, sc in each stitch.

Row 4: Turn, join Color B, drop Color A, ch1, sl st in flo of each stitch.

Row 5: Turn, fasten off Color B, pick up Color A, ch1, sc in blo of each stitch.

Row 6: Turn, ch1, sl st through both loops of each stitch.

Row 7: Turn, ch1, sc in blo of each stitch.

Row 8: Turn, ch2, hdc in each stitch.

Row 9: Turn, ch1, sc in each stitch.

Rows 10–15: Repeat Rows 8–9 three times.

Row 16: Repeat Row 8.

Round 17: Sl st to sixth stitch of opposite side of panel; turn, * 4sc, sc dec, repeat from * to complete round (54 sts).

Slip stitch to the sixth stitch of the opposite side of the panel. The hat will now be joined at the top. You will continue to decrease to form the crown of the hat.

Round 18: Working continuously in the round, * sc4, sc dec, repeat from * to complete round (45 sts).

Round 19: * Sc3, sc dec, repeat from * to complete round (36 sts).

Round 20: * Sc2, sc dec, repeat from * to complete round (27 sts).

Round 21: * Sc, sc dec, repeat from * to complete round (18 sts).

Round 22: * Sc dec, repeat from * to last stitch, sc in last stitch (9 sts).

Round 23: Sc in each stitch. Fasten off.
Weave yarn through last 9 stitches, pull tight. Fasten off. Weave in ends.

MEDIUM

Using Color A, ch71.

Row 1: Turn, sc in second chain from hook and in each chain across (70 sts).

Row 2: Turn, ch2, hdc in each stitch.

Row 3: Turn, ch1, sc in each stitch.

Row 4: Turn, join Color B, drop Color A, ch1, sl st in flo of each stitch.

Row 5: Turn, ch1, sc in blo of each stitch.

Row 6: Fasten off Color B, pick up Color A, turn, ch1, sl st through both loops of each stitch.

Row 7: Turn, ch1, sc in blo of each stitch.

Row 8: Turn, ch2, hdc in each stitch.

Row 9: Turn, ch1, sc in each stitch.

Rows 10–17: Repeat Rows 8–9 four times.

Row 18: Repeat Row 8.

Round 19: Sl st to sixth stitch of opposite side of panel; turn, * 7sc, sc dec, repeat from * to complete round (64 sts). (See photo at left.)

Round 20: Working continuously in the round, * sc6, sc dec, repeat from * to complete round (56 sts).

Round 21: * Sc5, sc dec, repeat from * to complete round (48 sts).

Round 22: * Sc4, sc dec, repeat from * to complete round (40 sts).

Round 23: * Sc3, sc dec, repeat from * to complete round (32 sts).

Round 24: * Sc2, sc dec, repeat from * to complete round (24 sts).

Round 25: * Sc, sc dec, repeat from * to complete round (16 sts).

Round 26: * Sc dec, repeat from * to complete round (8 sts).

Round 27: Sc in each stitch. Fasten off.

Weave yarn through last 8 stitches, pull tight. Fasten off. Weave in ends.

LARGE

Using Color A, ch81.

Row 1: Turn, sc in second chain from hook and in each chain across (80 sts).

Row 2: Turn, ch2, hdc in each stitch.

Row 3: Turn, ch1, sc in each stitch.

Rows 4–5: Repeat Rows 2–3.

Row 6: Turn, join Color B, drop Color A, ch1, sl st in flo of each stitch (80 sts).

Row 7: Turn, ch1, sc in blo of each stitch.

Row 8: Fasten off Color B, pick up Color A, turn, ch1, sl st through both loops of each stitch.

Row 9: Turn, ch1, sc in blo in each stitch.

Row 10: Turn, ch2, hdc in each stitch.

Row 11: Turn, ch1, sc in each stitch.

Rows 12–19: Repeat Rows 10–11 four times.

Row 20: Repeat Row 10.

Round 21: Sl st to eighth stitch of opposite side of panel; turn, * 7sc, sc dec, repeat from * to complete round (64 sts). (See photo on opposite page.)

Working along the side of the panel, use ends of rows as stitches. The ruffles will be added along the open side of the hat.

Round 22: Working continuously in the round, * sc6, sc dec, repeat from * to complete round (56 sts).

Round 23: * Sc5, sc dec, repeat from * to complete round (48 sts).

Round 24: * Sc4, sc dec, repeat from * to complete round (40 sts).

Round 25: * Sc3, sc dec, repeat from * to complete round (32 sts).

Round 26: * Sc2, sc dec, repeat from * to complete round (24 sts).

Round 27: * Sc, sc dec, repeat from * to complete round (16 sts).

Round 28: * Sc dec, repeat from * to complete round (8 sts).

Round 29: Sc in each stitch. Fasten off.

Weave yarn through last 8 stitches, pull tight. Fasten off. Weave in ends.

Trim

With right side out, join Color B at bottom left corner.

Ch1, bpsc in each stitch. When you reach opposite corner, 3sc in corner stitch.

Working along side of panel, use ends of rows as stitches.

(Sl st, ch3, sl st to same stitch) in each stitch along side of panel. At top corner, (sl st, ch3, sl st) in the corner stitch, and repeat across remaining stitches along the top of the flap.

Finishing

Using yarn needle, sew flap into place overlapping other side of hat. Weave in ends.

Using sewing needle and thread, sew buttons onto hat along edge of flap.

You Have My Heart Beanie

Every newborn baby, under-the-weather loved one, or special friend needs a heartfelt hat. This beanie sends the perfect message that they are loved and cherished.

Skill Level

Intermediate

Finished Measurements

Head circumference: X-Small: 12–14.5"/30.5–37 cm, Small: 15–17.5"/38–44.5 cm, Medium: 17.5–19"/44.5–48 cm, Large: 19–22.5"/48–57 cm
Height: X-Small: 4.5–6"/11.5–15 cm, Small: 6–6.5"/15–16.5 cm, Medium: 6.5–7"/16.5–18 cm, Large: 7–7.5"/18–19 cm

Yarn

* Red Heart Soft, medium worsted weight #4 yarn (100% acrylic; 256 yd/5 oz, 234 m/142 g per skein)
    1 skein #4601 Off White (Color A)
    1 skein #9925 Really Red (Color B)

Hook and Other Materials

* F-5 (3.75 mm) hook or size to obtain gauge
* H-8 (5.0 mm) hook or size to obtain gauge (for Medium size only)
* Yarn needle

Gauge

Using F-5 (3.75 mm) hook: 16 sts and 18 rows in sc = 4"/10 cm square
Using H-8 (5.0 mm) hook: 14 sts and 16 rows in sc = 4"10 cm square

Notes

1. The hat is worked in sections: the row of hearts is made first, then the beanie is crocheted on top of that, then the brim is worked from the bottom of the heart row.
2. You will make one Heart 1 to begin the beanie, and then the remaining hearts use the Heart 2 pattern as they will join together each time.
3. See page 126 for a tutorial on Single Crochet Decrease (sc dec) and page 124 for crocheting into the Back Loop Only (blo).

Special Techniques

Heart 1

Using Color B, ch2.
Row 1: Turn, 2sc in second chain from hook (2 sts).
Row 2: Turn, ch1, 2sc in each stitch (4 sts).
Row 3: Turn, ch1, 2sc, sc2, 2sc (6 sts).
Row 4: Turn, ch1, 2sc, sc4, 2sc (8 sts).
Row 5: Turn, ch1, sc in each stitch.
Top of heart part 1:
Row 6: Turn, ch1, sc4 (4 sts).
Row 7: Turn, sc dec, sc dec (2 sts).
Row 8: Turn, sc dec (1 st).
Fasten off.
Top of heart part 2:
Row 6 : Join yarn in fifth stitch of Row 5, sc 4 (4 sts)
Row 7: Turn, sc dec, sc dec (2 sts).
Row 8: Turn, sc dec (1 st).
Fasten off. Weave in ends.

Heart 2

Using Color B, ch2.
Row 1: Turn, 2sc in second chain from hook (2 sts).
Row 2: Turn, ch1, 2sc in each stitch (4 sts).
Row 3: Turn, ch1, 2sc, sc2, 2sc (6 sts).
Row 4: Turn, ch1, 2sc, sc4, 2sc (8 sts).
Row 5: Turn, ch1, sc7, using last stitch of row and end of Row 5 of previous heart, sc dec to join hearts together, flipping previous heart as necessary so hearts alternate up and down (8 sts).
Top of heart part 1:
Row 6: Turn, ch1, sc4 (4 sts).
Row 7: Turn, sc dec, sc dec (2 sts).
Row 8: Turn, sc dec (1 st).
Fasten off.
Top of heart part 2:
Row 6: Join yarn in fifth stitch of Row 5, sc 4 (4 sts)
Row 7: Turn, sc dec, sc dec (2 sts).
Row 8: Turn, sc dec (1 st).
Fasten off. Weave in ends.

Hat

X-SMALL

Using F-5 (3.75 mm) hook and Color B, work Heart 1 one time and Heart 2 seven times, joining as you go as directed, for a total of 8 hearts. Using yarn needle, sew first and last hearts together on Row 5 of the hearts.

Round 1: Join Color A at bottom point of any heart, *ch4, sl st to top of part 1 of next heart, ch4, sl st to top of part 2 of same heart, ch5, sl st to point of next heart, repeat from * around.

Round 2: Working continuously in the round, sc in blo of each chain and sl st (64 sts).

Rounds 3–8: Sc in each stitch.

Round 9: * Sc6, sc dec, repeat from * to complete round (56 sts).

Round 10: * Sc5, sc dec, repeat from * to complete round (48 sts).

Round 11: * Sc4, sc dec, repeat from * to complete round (40 sts).

Round 12: * Sc3, sc dec, repeat from * to complete round (32 sts).

Round 13: * Sc2, sc dec, repeat from * to complete round (24 sts).

Round 14: * Sc, sc dec repeat from * to complete round (16 sts).

Round 15: Sc dec 8 times (8 sts).

Round 16: Sc in each stitch, sl st to first stitch of round to join.

Fasten off, leaving a long tail to close top. Using yarn needle, weave tail in and out of last row, pull tight, and fasten off. Weave in ends.

SMALL

Using F-5 (3.75 mm) hook and Color B, work Heart 1 one time and Heart 2 nine times, joining as you go as directed, for a total of 10 hearts. Using yarn needle, sew the first and last hearts together on Row 5 of the hearts.

Round 1: Join Color A at bottom point of any heart, *ch4, sl st to top of part 1 of next heart, ch4, sl st to top of part 2 of same heart, ch5, sl st to point of next heart, repeat from * around.

Round 2: Working continuously in the round, sc in blo of each chain and sl st (80 sts).

Rounds 3–10: Sc in each stitch.

Round 11: * Sc8, sc dec, repeat from * to complete round (72 sts).

Round 12: * Sc7, sc dec, repeat from * to complete round (64 sts).

Round 13: * Sc6, sc dec, repeat from * to complete round (56 sts).

Round 14: * Sc5, sc dec, repeat from * to complete round (48 sts).

Round 15: * Sc4, sc dec, repeat from * to complete round (40 sts).

Round 16: * Sc3, sc dec, repeat from * to complete round (32 sts).

Round 17: * Sc2, sc dec, repeat from * to complete round (24 sts).

Round 18: * Sc, sc dec repeat from * to complete round (16 sts).

Round 19: Sc dec 8 times (8 sts).

Round 20: Sc in each stitch, sl st to first stitch of round to join.

Fasten off, leaving a long tail to close top. Using yarn needle, weave tail in and out of last row, pull tight, and fasten off. Weave in ends.

MEDIUM

Using H-8 (5.0 mm) hook, work Small size pattern. Using the larger hook will naturally increase the gauge and size.

LARGE

Using F-5 (3.75 mm) hook and Color B, work Heart 1 one time and Heart 2 eleven times, joining as you go as directed, for a total of 12 hearts. Using yarn needle, sew first and last hearts together on Row 5 of the hearts.

Round 1: Join Color A at bottom point of any heart, *ch4, sl st to top of part 1 of next heart, ch4, sl st to top of part 2 of same heart, ch5, sl st to point of next heart, repeat from * around.

Round 2: Working continuously in the round, sc in blo of each chain and sl st (96 sts).

Rounds 3–14: Sc in each stitch.

Round 15: * Sc10, sc dec, repeat from * to complete round (88 sts).

Round 16: * Sc9, sc dec, repeat from * to complete round (80 sts).

Round 17: * Sc8, sc dec, repeat from * to complete round (72 sts).

Round 18: * Sc7, sc dec, repeat from * to complete round (64 sts).

Round 19: * Sc6, sc dec, repeat from * to complete round (56 sts).

Round 20: * Sc5, sc dec, repeat from * to complete round (48 sts).

Round 21: * Sc4, sc dec, repeat from * to complete round (40 sts).

Round 22: * Sc3, sc dec, repeat from * to complete round (32 sts).

Round 23: * Sc2, sc dec, repeat from * to complete round (24 sts).

Round 24: * Sc, sc dec repeat from * to complete round (16 sts).

Round 25: Sc dec 8 times (8 sts).

Round 26: Sc in each stitch, sl st to first stitch of round to join.

Fasten off, leaving a long tail to close top. Using yarn needle, weave tail in and out of last row, pull tight, and fasten off. Weave in ends.

Brim

Row 1: Using the same size hook as for the rest of the hat, join Color A at bottom point of any heart, ch4.

Row 2: Turn, sc in second chain from hook and next 2 chains.

Rows 3–7: Turn, sc3 (3 sts).

Row 8: Turn, sc2, sc2tog in next st and top of part 1 of next heart (3 sts).

Rows 9–11: Turn, sc3.

Row 12: Turn, sc2, sc2tog in next st and top of part 2 of next heart (3 sts).

Rows 13–19; Turn, sc3.

Row 20: Turn, sc2, sc2tog in next st and point of next heart (3 sts).

Rows 21–22: Turn, sc 3.

Repeat rows 3–22 around the hat, ending with a row 20 joining to the point of the heart where you started.

Using yarn needle, sew first and last rows together to join.

Fasten off. Weave in ends.

The brim will be worked sideways and attached to the heart points and tops as you go. This will allow the beanie to stretch around the head instead of being pulled tight.

Snowman Hat

Let it snow! Let it snow! Let it snow! Keep warm inside and crochet a snowman hat!

Skill Level

Beginner

Finished Measurements

Head circumference: X-Small: 12–14.5"/30.5–37 cm, Small: 15–17.5"/38–44.5 cm, Medium: 17.5–19"/44.5–48 cm, Large: 19–22.5"/48–57 cm, X-Large: 23–24.5"/58–62 cm
Height: X-Small: 4.5–6"/11.5–15 cm, Small: 6–6.5"/15–16.5 cm, Medium: 6.5–7"/16.5–18 cm, Large: 7–7.5"/18–19 cm, X-Large: 7.5–8"/19–20.5 cm

Yarn

- Bernat Soft Boucle, light weight #3 yarn (100% acrylic; 144 yd/5.75 oz, 132 m/136 g per skein)
    2 skeins #46008 Natural (Color A)
- Lion Brand Vanna's Choice, medium worsted weight #4 yarn (100% acrylic; 170 yd/3.5 oz, 156 m/100 g per skein)
    1 skein #860-180 Cranberry (Color B)
    1 skein #860-172 Kelly Green (Color C)
    1 skein #860-135 Rust (Color D)

Hook and Other Materials

- N-13 (9.0 mm) hook or size to obtain gauge
- H-8 (5.0 mm) hook or size to obtain gauge
- Fiberfill
- Yarn needle
- 2 medium black buttons
- Sewing thread and needle

Gauge

Using N-13 (9.0 mm) hook and 2 strands of Color A together: 7 sts and 5 rows in dc = 4"/10 cm square
Using H-8 (5.0 mm) hook and Color B, C, or D: 16 sts and 16 rows in sc = 4"/10 cm square

Notes

1. The hat is worked from the top down in rounds.
2. The earmuffs are crocheted separately and sewn onto the hat.
3. You will work with 2 strands of Color A held together to crochet the main part of the hat. The earmuffs and nose will be crocheted with only one strand.
4. The ch2 at beginning of rounds of the hat does not count as a stitch.
5. See page 124 for a tutorial on crocheting into Back Loop Only (blo) and Front Loop Only (flo).

Hat

X-SMALL

Using N-13 (9.0 mm) hook and 2 strands of Color A together, ch4, sl st to first chain to form a ring.
Round 1: Ch2, 8dc in ring, sl st to first stitch to join round (8 sts).
Round 2: Ch2, 2dc in each stitch, sl st to first stitch to join (16 sts).
Round 3: Ch2, * dc, 2dc in next stitch, repeat from * to complete round, sl st to first stitch to join (24 sts).
Rounds 4–7: Ch2, dc in each stitch, sl st to first stitch to join.
Fasten off. Weave in ends.

SMALL

Using N-13 (9.0 mm) hook and 2 strands of Color A together, ch4, sl st to first chain to form a ring.
Round 1: Ch2, 10dc in ring, sl st to first stitch to join round (10 sts).
Round 2: Ch2, 2dc in each stitch, sl st to first stitch to join (20 sts).
Round 3: Ch2, * dc, 2dc in next stitch, repeat from * to complete round, sl st to first stitch to join (30 sts).
Rounds 4–8: Ch2, dc in each stitch, sl st to first stitch to join.
Fasten off. Weave in ends.

MEDIUM

Using N-13 (9.0 mm) hook and 2 strands of Color A together, ch4, sl st to first chain to form a ring.
Round 1: Ch2, 11dc in ring, sl st to first stitch to join round (11 sts).
Round 2: Ch2, 2dc in each stitch, sl st to first stitch to join (22 sts).
Round 3: Ch2, * dc, 2dc in next stitch, repeat from * to complete round, sl st to first stitch to join (33 sts).
Rounds 4–9: Ch2, dc in each stitch, sl st to first stitch to join.
Fasten off. Weave in ends.

LARGE

Using N-13 (9.0 mm) hook and 2 strands of Color A together, ch4, sl st to first chain to form a ring.
Round 1: Ch2, 10dc in ring, sl st to first stitch to join round (10 sts).
Round 2: Ch2, 2dc in each stitch, sl st to first stitch to join (20 sts).
Round 3: Ch2, * dc, 2dc in next stitch, repeat from * to complete round, sl st to first stitch to join (30 sts).

Round 4: Ch2, * dc2, 2dc in next stitch, repeat from * to complete round, sl st to first stitch to join (40 sts).
Rounds 5–10: Ch2, dc in each stitch, sl st to first stitch to join.
Fasten off. Weave in ends.

X-LARGE

Using N-13 (9.0 mm) hook and 2 strands of Color A held together, ch4, sl st to first chain to form a ring.
Round 1: Ch2, 9dc in ring, sl st to first stitch to join (9 sts).
Round 2: Ch2, 2dc in each stitch, sl st to first stitch to join round (18 sts).
Round 3: Ch2, * dc, 2dc in next stitch, repeat from * to complete round, sl st to first stitch to join (27 sts).
Round 4: Ch2, * dc2, 2dc in next stitch, repeat from * to complete round, sl st to first stitch to join (36 sts).
Round 5: Ch2, * dc3, 2dc in next stitch, repeat from * to complete round, sl st to first stitch to join (45 sts).
Rounds 6–11: Ch2, dc in each stitch, sl st to first stitch to join.
Fasten off. Weave in ends.

Earmuffs (make 2)

X-SMALL, SMALL & MEDIUM

Using H-8 (5.0 mm) hook and Color B or C, ch2.
Round 1: 6sc in second chain from hook (6 sts).
Round 2: Working continuously in the round, 2sc in each stitch (12 sts).
Round 3: * Sc, 2sc in next stitch, repeat from * to complete round (18 sts).
Round 4: * Sc2, 2sc in next stitch, repeat from * to complete round (24 sts).
Round 5: * Sc3, 2sc in next stitch, repeat from * to complete round (30 sts).
Rounds 6–10: Sc in each stitch.
To finish, sl st to first stitch of round to join. Fasten off, leaving a long tail to sew onto hat.

LARGE & X-LARGE

Using H-8 (5.0 mm) hook and Color B or C, ch2.

Round 1: 6sc in second chain from hook (6 sts).

Round 2: Working continuously in the round, 2sc in each stitch (12 sts).

Round 3: * Sc, 2sc in next stitch, repeat from * to complete round (18 sts).

Round 4: * Sc2, 2sc in next stitch, repeat from * to complete round (24 sts).

Round 5: * Sc3, 2sc in next stitch, repeat from * to complete round (30 sts).

Round 6: * Sc4, 2sc in next stitch, repeat from * to complete round (36 sts).

Rounds 7–12: Sc in each stitch.

To finish, sl st to first stitch of round to join. Fasten off, leaving a long tail to sew onto hat.

Nose

Using H-8 (5.0 mm) hook and Color D, ch2.

Round 1: 3sc in second chain from hook (3 sts).

Round 2: Working continuously in the round, 2sc in each stitch (6 sts).

Round 3: * Sc, 2sc in next stitch (9 sts).

Rounds 4–8: Sc in each stitch.

Fasten off, leaving a long tail to sew onto hat.

Finishing

Using sewing needle and thread, sew buttons onto hat as eyes.

Using yarn needle, sew nose onto hat.

Stuff the earmuffs with fiberfil and sew onto each side of hat.

After sewing earmuffs on, add headband.

NOTE: Depending on placement of ear muffs, you may need to increase or decrease number of rows in the headband.

On right earmuff, join Color B or C 3 stitches to right of top center stitch using size H-8 (5.0 mm) hook.

Row 1: Ch3 (counts as first dc), dc6 (7 sts).

Row 2: Turn, ch3, dc in blo of each stitch.

Row 3: Turn, ch3, dc in flo of each stitch.

Rows 4–13: Repeat Rows 2–3 five times.

When the headband reaches the other earmuff without stretching, sew band onto last row of other earmuff using yarn needle. Fasten off. Weave in ends.

Gone Huntin' Camo Cap

This camo-pattern cap makes a great gift for a hunting dad and his kids (or a hunting mom). Or crochet it in a solid and see the amazing texture appear! You will love making this hat for boys and girls!

Skill Level

Intermediate

Finished Measurements

Head circumference: Small: 15–17.5"/38–44.5, Medium: 17.5–19"/44.5–48 cm, Large: 19–22.5"/48–57 cm, X-Large: 23–24.5"/58.5–62 cm
Height: Small: 6–6.5"/15–16.5 cm, Medium: 6.5–7"/ 44.5–48 cm, Large: 7–7.5"/48–57 cm, X-Large: 7.5–8"/ 58.5–62xm

Yarn

• Red Heart Super Saver, medium worsted weight #4 yarn (100% acrylic; 364 yd/7 oz, 333 m/199 g per skein)
  1 skein #0971 Camouflage

Hook and Other Materials

• F-5 (3.75 mm) hook or size to obtain gauge (for Small and Medium sizes only)
• N-13 (9.0 mm) hook or size to obtain gauge (for Large and X-Large sizes only)
• Stitch markers
• Yarn needle

Gauge

Using F-5 (3.75 mm) hook, 16 sts and 18 rows in sc = 4"/10 cm square
Using N-13 (9.0 mm) hook, 10 sts and 12 rows in sc = 4"/10 cm square

Notes

1. The hat is worked from the top down continuously in the round. If you like, you can use a stitch marker to mark the first stitch of each round for reference.
2. The brim is crocheted directly onto the last row of the hat.

Special Techniques
Back Post Single Crochet (bpsc)

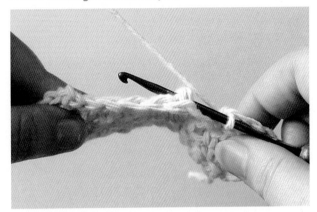

1 Insert hook from back to front to back of the stitch around the post.

2 Yarn over and pull yarn back around post: 2 loops on hook

3 Yarn over and draw yarn through both loops on hook to complete.

Back Post Single Crochet Decrease (bpsc dec)

A back post single crochet decrease will take two stitches and make them into one stitch using the posts.

1 Insert hook around the post of the stitch from back to front to back.

2 Yarn over and pull yarn back around post—2 loops on hook.

3 Insert hook around the post of the next stitch from back to front to back, yarn over, and pull yarn back around post—3 loops on hook.

4 Yarn over and draw through all loops on hook to complete the stitch.

Hat

SMALL

Using F-5 (3.75 mm) hook, ch4, sl st to first chain to create a ring.
Round 1: Ch1, 10sc in ring (10 sts).
Round 2: Working continuously in the round, 2bpsc (see Special Techniques) in each stitch (20 sts).
Round 3: * Bpsc, 2bpsc in next stitch, repeat from * to complete round (30 sts).

Round 4: * Bpsc2, 2bpsc in next stitch, repeat from * to complete round (40 sts).
Round 5: * Bpsc3, 2bpsc in next stitch, repeat from * to complete round (50 sts).
Round 6: * Bpsc4, 2bpsc in next stitch, repeat from * to complete round (60 sts).
Round 7: * Bpsc5, 2bpsc in next stitch, repeat from * to complete round (70 sts).
Round 8: * Bpsc6, 2bpsc in next stitch, repeat from * to complete round (80 sts).
Round 9: * Bpsc7, 2bpsc in next stitch, repeat from * to complete round (90 sts).
Rounds 10–16: Bpsc in each stitch.
Rounds 17–19: Sc in each stitch.
To finish, sl st to first stitch of round. Fasten off. Weave in ends.

MEDIUM

Using F-5 (3.75 mm) hook, ch4, sl st to first chain to create a ring.
Round 1: Ch1, 10sc in ring (10 sts).
Round 2: Working continuously in the round, 2bpsc (see Special Techniques) in each stitch (20 sts).
Round 3: * Bpsc, 2bpsc in next stitch, repeat from * to complete round (30 sts).
Round 4: * Bpsc2, 2bpsc in next stitch, repeat from * to complete round (40 sts).

Round 5: * Bpsc3, 2bpsc in next stitch, repeat from * to complete round (50 sts).
Round 6: * Bpsc4, 2bpsc in next stitch, repeat from * to complete round (60 sts).
Round 7: * Bpsc5, 2bpsc in next stitch, repeat from * to complete round (70 sts).
Round 8: * Bpsc6, 2bpsc in next stitch, repeat from * to complete round (80 sts).
Round 9: * Bpsc7, 2bpsc in next stitch, repeat from * to complete round (90 sts).
Round 10: * Bpsc8, 2bpsc in next stitch, repeat from * to complete round (100 sts).
Round 11: * Bpsc9, 2bpsc in next stitch, repeat from * to complete round (110 sts).
Rounds 12–19: Bpsc in each stitch.
Rounds 20–21: Sc in each stitch.
To finish, sl st to first stitch of round. Fasten off. Weave in ends.

LARGE

Using N-13 (9.0 mm) hook, ch4, sl st to first chain to create a ring.
Round 1: Ch1, 10sc in ring (10 sts).
Round 2: Working continuously in the round, 2bpsc (see Special Techniques) in each stitch (20 sts).
Round 3: * Bpsc, 2bpsc in next stitch, repeat from * to complete round (30 sts).
Round 4: * Bpsc2, 2bpsc in next stitch, repeat from * to complete round (40 sts).
Round 5: * Bpsc3, 2bpsc in next stitch, repeat from * to complete round (50 sts).
Round 6: * Bpsc4, 2bpsc in next stitch, repeat from * to complete round (60 sts).
Round 7: * Bpsc5, 2bpsc in next stitch, repeat from * to complete round (70 sts).
Rounds 8–16: Bpsc in each stitch.
Round 17: * Bpsc8, bpsc dec (see Special Techniques), repeat from * to complete round (63 sts).
Rounds 18–19: Bpsc in each stitch.
Rounds 20–23: Sc in each stitch.
To finish, sl st to first stitch of round. Fasten off. Weave in ends.

X-LARGE

Using N-13 (9.0 mm) hook, ch4, sl st to first chain to create a ring.
Round 1: Ch1, 10sc in ring (10 sts).
Round 2: Working continuously in the round, 2bpsc (see Special Techniques) in each stitch (20 sts).
Round 3: * Bpsc, 2bpsc in next stitch, repeat from * to complete round (30 sts).
Round 4: * Bpsc2, 2bpsc in next stitch, repeat from * to complete round (40 sts).
Round 5: * Bpsc3, 2bpsc in next stitch, repeat from * to complete round (50 sts).
Round 6: * Bpsc4, 2bpsc in next stitch, repeat from * to complete round (60 sts).

Round 7: * Bpsc5, 2bpsc in next stitch, repeat from * to complete round (70 sts).
Round 8: * Bpsc6, 2bpsc in next stitch, repeat from * to complete round (80 sts).
Round 9: * Bpsc7, 2bpsc in next stitch, repeat from * to complete round (90 sts).
Rounds 10–18: Bpsc in each stitch.
Round 19: * Bpsc8, bpsc dec (see Special Techniques), repeat from * to complete round (81 sts).
Rounds 20–21: Bpsc in each stitch.
Rounds 22–24: Sc in each stitch.
To finish, sl st to first stitch of round. Fasten off. Weave in ends.

Brim

SMALL

Using F-5 (3.75 mm) hook, join yarn in any stitch in last round.
Row 1: Ch1, sc45 across stitches of last row (45 sts).
Rows 2–4: Turn, ch1, sc to end of row.
Row 5: Turn, sc dec, sc41, sc dec (43 sts).
Row 6: Turn, sc dec, sc39, sc dec (41 sts).
Row 7: Turn, sc dec, sc37, sc dec (39 sts).
Fasten off. Weave in ends.

MEDIUM

Using F-5 (3.75 mm) hook, join yarn in any stitch in last round.
Row 1: Ch1, sc50 across stitches of last row (50 sts).
Rows 2–4: Turn, ch1, sc to end of row.
Row 5: Turn, sc dec, sc46, sc dec (48 sts).
Row 6: Turn, sc dec, sc44, sc dec (46 sts).
Row 7: Turn, sc dec, sc42, sc dec (44 sts).
Fasten off. Weave in ends.

LARGE

Using N-13 (9.0 mm) hook, join yarn in any stitch in last round.
Row 1: Ch1, sc35 across stitches of last row (35 sts).
Rows 2–3: Turn, ch1, sc to end of row.
Row 4: Turn, sc dec, sc31, sc dec (33 sts).
Row 5: Turn, sc dec, sc29, sc dec (31 sts).
Row 6: Turn, sc dec, sc27, sc dec (29 sts).
Fasten off. Weave in ends.

X-LARGE

Using N-13 (9.0 mm) hook, join yarn in any stitch in last round.
Row 1: Ch1, sc40 across stitches of last row (40 sts).
Rows 2–3: Turn, ch1, sc to end of row.
Row 4: Turn, sc dec, sc36, sc dec (38 sts).
Row 5: Turn, sc dec, sc34, sc dec (36 sts).
Row 6: Turn, sc dec, sc32, sc dec (34 sts).
Fasten off. Weave in ends.

Pigtail Hat

This little piggy loved pigtails. This little piggy wanted a hat. Mommy loved to crochet and made one stat! This fun design with two openings to pull your pigtails through is sure to bring smiles to everyone around!

Skill Level

Beginner

Finished Measurements

Head circumference: Small: 15–17.5"/38–44.5 cm, Medium: 17.5–19"/44.5–48 cm, Large: 19–22.5"/48–57 cm

Yarn

- Peaches & Creme, medium worsted weight #4 yarn (100% cotton; 120 yd/2.5 oz, 110 m/71 g per skein)
    1 skein #1628 Bright Orange (Color A)
    1 skein #1740 Bright Pink (Color B)
    1 skein #1612 Sunshine (Color C)
    1 skein #1318 Black Currant (Color D)
    1 skein #1005 White (Color E)
- Lily Sugar'n Cream, medium worsted weight #4 yarn (100% cotton; 200 yd/4 oz, 138 m/114 g per skein)
    1 skein #1712 Hot Green (Color F)

Hook and Other Materials

- H-8 (5.0 mm) hook or size needed to obtain gauge
- 1 medium button
- Sewing thread and needle

Gauge

12 sts and 8 rows in dc = 4"/10 cm square

Notes

1. The hat is worked in rounds from the top down.
2. The ch2 or ch1 at the beginning of each round is not counted as a stitch.
3. To change colors, push hook through the last stitch of the first color, pull yarn back through, yarn over with the NEXT color, and pull through. Color change is complete. Also see page 131 for a tutorial.
4. See page 131 for a tutorial on Treble Crochet (tr).

Hat

SMALL

Using Color A, ch2.

Round 1: 8dc in second chain from hook, sl st to first stitch to join round (8 sts).

Round 2: Fasten off Color A, join Color B, ch2, 2dc in each stitch, sl st to first stitch to join (16 sts).

Round 3: Fasten off Color B, join Color F, ch1, * sc, 2sc in next stitch, repeat from * to complete round, sl st to first stitch to join (24 sts).

Round 4: Fasten off Color F, join Color C, ch2, * dc2, 2dc in next stitch, repeat from * to complete round, sl st to first stitch to join (32 sts).

Round 5: Fasten off Color C, join Color D, ch2, * dc3, 2dc in next stitch, repeat from * to complete round, sl st to first stitch to join (40 sts).

Round 6: Fasten off Color D, join Color A, ch1, * sc4, 2sc in next stitch, repeat from * to complete round, sl st to first stitch to join (48 sts).

Round 7: Fasten off Color A, join Color B, ch2, dc in each stitch, sl st to first stitch to join.

Round 8: Fasten off Color B, join Color F, ch2, dc11, ch4, skip next 4 stitches, dc19, ch4, skip next 4 stitches, dc11, sl st to first stitch to join.

Each ch4 (or ch5 for adult) will create a space for the pigtail on each side of the hat.

Round 9: Fasten off Color F, join Color C, ch1, sc in each stitch, sl st to first stitch to join.

Round 10: Fasten off Color C, join Color D, ch2, dc in each stitch, sl st to first stitch to join.

Round 11: Fasten off Color D, join Color A, ch2, dc in each stitch, sl st to first stitch to join.

Round 12: Fasten off Color A, join Color B, ch1, sc in each stitch, sl st to first stitch to join.
Round 13: Fasten off Color B, join Color F, ch2, dc in each stitch, sl st to first stitch to join.
Round 14: Fasten off Color F, join Color E, ch1, sc in each stitch, sl st to first stitch to join.
Rounds 15–16: Ch1, sc in each stitch, sl st to first stitch to join.
Fasten off. Weave in ends.

MEDIUM

Using Color A, ch2.
Round 1: 8dc in second chain from hook, sl st to first stitch to join round (8 sts).
Round 2: Fasten off Color A, join Color B, ch2, 2dc in each stitch, sl st to first stitch to join (16 sts).
Round 3: Fasten off Color B, join Color F, ch1, * sc, 2sc in next stitch, repeat from * to complete round, sl st to first stitch to join (24 sts).
Round 4: Fasten off Color F, join Color C, ch2, * dc2, 2dc in next stitch, repeat from * to complete round, sl st to first stitch to join (32 sts).
Round 5: Fasten off Color C, join Color D, ch2, * dc3, 2dc in next stitch, repeat from * to complete round, sl st to first stitch to join (40 sts).

Round 6: Fasten off Color D, join Color A, ch1, * sc4, 2sc in next stitch, repeat from * to complete round, sl st to first stitch to join (48 sts).
Round 7: Fasten off Color A, join Color B, ch2, * dc5, 2dc in each stitch, sl st to first stitch to join (54 sts).
Round 8: Fasten off Color B, join Color F, ch1, sc in each stitch, sl st to first stitch to join.
Round 9: Fasten off Color F, join Color C, ch2, dc11, ch4, skip next 4 stitches, dc23, ch4, skip next 4 stitches, dc12, sl st to first stitch to join.
Round 10: Fasten off Color C, join Color D, ch2, dc in each stitch, sl st to first stitch to join.
Round 11: Fasten off Color D, join Color A, ch1, sc in each stitch, sl st to first stitch to join.
Round 12: Fasten off Color A, join Color B, ch2, dc in each stitch, sl st to first stitch to join.
Round 13: Fasten off Color B, join Color F, ch2, dc in each stitch, sl st to first stitch to join.
Round 14: Fasten off Color F, join Color A, ch1, sc in each stitch, sl st to first stitch to join.
Round 15: Fasten off Color A, join Color E, ch1, sc in each stitch, sl st to first stitch to join.
Rounds 16–17: Ch1, sc in each stitch, sl st to first stitch to join.
Fasten off. Weave in ends.

Round 8: Fasten off Color B, join Color F, ch2, dc14, ch5, skip next 5 stitches, dc27, ch5, skip next 5 stitches, dc15, sl st to first stitch to join.

Round 9: Fasten off Color F, join Color C, ch1, sc in each stitch, sl st to first stitch to join.

Round 10: Fasten off Color C, join Color D, ch2, dc in each stitch, sl st to first stitch to join.

Round 11: Fasten off Color D, join Color A, ch2, dc in each stitch, sl st to first stitch to join.

Round 12: Fasten off Color A, join Color B, ch1, * sc8, sc dec, repeat from * to last 6 stitches, sc6, sl st to first stitch to join (60 sts).

Round 13: Fasten off Color B, join Color F, ch2, dc in each stitch, sl st to first stitch to join.

Round 14: Fasten off Color F, join Color C, ch2, dc in each stitch, sl st to first stitch to join.

Round 15: Fasten off Color C, join Color D, ch1, sc in each stitch, sl st to first stitch to join.

Round 16: Fasten off Color D, join Color E, ch1, sc in each stitch, sl st to first stitch to join.

Rounds 17–19: Ch1, sc in each stitch, sl st to first stitch to join.

Fasten off. Weave in ends.

Flower

Using Color B, ch4, sl st to first chain to create a ring.

Round 1: Ch1, 8sc in ring, sl st to first stitch to join round (8 sts).

Round 2: Fasten off Color B, join Color E, (ch1, dc, tr, dc, ch1, sl st) in same stitch as joining, * (sl st, ch1, dc, tr, dc, ch1, sl st) in next stitch, repeat from * to complete 8 petals. To finish, sl st to first ch1 to join.

Fasten off. Weave in ends.

Finishing

With sewing needle and thread, sew button onto hat. Slip center of flower over button.

LARGE

Using Color A, ch2.

Round 1: 11dc in second chain from hook, sl st to first stitch to join round (11 sts).

Round 2: Fasten off Color A, join Color B, ch2, 2dc in each stitch, sl st to first stitch to join (22 sts).

Round 3: Fasten off Color B, join Color F, ch1, * sc, 2sc in next stitch, repeat from * to complete round, sl st to first stitch to join (33 sts).

Round 4: Fasten off Color F, join Color C, ch2, * dc2, 2dc in next stitch, repeat from * to complete round, sl st to first stitch to join (44 sts).

Round 5: Fasten off Color C, join Color D, ch2, * dc3, 2dc in next stitch, repeat from * to complete round, sl st to first stitch to join (55 sts).

Round 6: Fasten off Color D, join Color A, ch1, * sc4, 2sc in next stitch, repeat from * to complete round, sl st to first stitch to join (66 sts).

Round 7: Fasten off Color A, join Color B, ch2, dc in each stitch, sl st to first stitch to join.

Thick and Thin Hat

f you're looking for a super soft hat with a unique look, then this is the one for you. Crocheting with thick and thin yarn is a treat and I promise this yarn and pattern will not disappoint!

Skill Level

Beginner

Finished Measurements

Head circumference: X-Small: 12–14.5"/30.5–37 cm, Small: 15–17.5"/38–44.5 cm, Medium: 17.5–19"/44.5–48 cm, Large: 19–22.5"/48–57 cm, X-Large: 23–24.5"/58.5–62 cm
Height: X-Small: 4.5–6"/11.5–15 cm, Small: 6–6.5"/15–16.5 cm, Medium: 6.5–7"/16.5–18 cm, Large: 7–7.5"/18–19 cm, X-Large: 7.5–8"/19–20.5 cm

Yarn

• Heartstrings By Dee Thick and Thin (www.HeartstringsbyDee.etsy.com), super bulky weight #6 yarn (100% merino; 70 yd/4.2 oz, 64 m/4 g per skein)
    1 skein Plum Craze (Color A)
    1 skein Lagoon (Color B)

Hook and Other Materials

• N-13 (9.0 mm) hook or size to obtain gauge
• 1 small and 1 large button (optional)
• Sewing needle and thread

Gauge

9 sts and 14 rows in sc = 4"/10 cm square

Notes

1. The hat is worked from the top down in rounds.
2. When using the thick and thin yarn, work loosely so that the texture stays intact. If the yarn is pulled tight, the texture will not be seen.
3. The ch1 or ch2 *at the beginning* of each round does not count as a stitch. The ch1 *within* rounds that skip stitches is counted as a stitch.
4. See page 124 for a tutorial on crocheting into the Back Loop Only (blo) and page 126 for Single Crochet Decrease (sc dec).

Hat

X-SMALL

Using Color A, ch4.
Round 1: 10dc in fourth chain from hook, sl st to first stitch to join round (10 sts).
Round 2: Ch1, (sc, dc) in each stitch, sl st to first stitch to join (20 sts).
Round 3: Ch2, * (hdc, dc) in next stitch, sc, 2dc, repeat from * to complete round, sl st to first stitch to join (25 sts).
Round 4: Ch2, * dc, sc, hdc, repeat from * to complete round, sl st to first stitch to join.
Round 5: Ch1, * sc, dc, ch1, skip 1 stitch, dc in next stitch, hdc, repeat from * to complete round, sl st to first stitch to join.
Rounds 6–9: Repeat Rounds 4–5 twice.
Round 10: Join Color C, fasten off Color A, ch1, sc in blo of each stitch.
Rounds 11–13: Working continuously in the round, sc in each stitch.
To finish, sl st to first stitch of round to join. Fasten off. Weave in ends.

SMALL

Using Color A, ch4.

Round 1: 10dc in fourth chain from hook, sl st to first stitch to join round (10 sts).

Round 2: Ch1, (sc, dc) in each stitch, sl st to first stitch to join (20 sts).

Round 3: Ch2, * dc, (hdc, dc) in next stitch, repeat from * to complete round, sl st to first stitch to join (30 sts).

Round 4: Ch2, * dc, sc, hdc, repeat from * to complete round, sl st to first stitch to join.

Round 5: Ch1, * sc, dc, ch1, skip 1 stitch, dc in next stitch, hdc, repeat from * to complete round, sl st to first stitch to join.

Rounds 6–9: Repeat Rounds 4–5 twice.

Round 10: Join Color C, fasten off Color A, ch1, sc in blo of each stitch.

Rounds 11–14: Working continuously in the round, sc in each stitch.

To finish, sl st to first stitch of round to join. Fasten off. Weave in ends.

MEDIUM

Using Color A, ch4.

Round 1: 10dc in fourth chain from hook, sl st to first stitch to join round (10 sts).

Round 2: Ch1, (sc, dc) in each stitch, sl st to first stitch to join (20 sts).

Round 3: Ch2, * dc, (hdc, dc) in next stitch, repeat from * to complete round, sl st to first stitch to join (30 sts).

Round 4: Ch2, * dc, sc, ch1, skip 1 stitch, dc, 2hdc in next stitch, repeat from * to complete round, sl st to first stitch to join (36 sts).

Round 5: Ch2, * dc, sc, hdc, repeat from * to complete round, sl st to first stitch to join.

Round 6: Ch1, * sc, 2dc, ch1, skip 1 stitch, dc in next stitch, hdc, repeat from * to complete round, sl st to first stitch to join.

Rounds 7–10: Repeat Rounds 4–5 twice.

Round 11: Join Color C, fasten off Color A, ch1, sc in blo of each stitch.

Round 12: Working continuously in the round, * sc4, sc dec, repeat from * to complete round (30 sts)

Rounds 13–15: Sc in each stitch.

To finish, sl st to first stitch of round to join. Fasten off. Weave in ends.

LARGE

Using Color B, ch4.

Round 1: 10dc in fourth chain from hook, sl st to first stitch to join round (10 sts).

Round 2: Ch1, (sc, dc) in each stitch, sl st to first stitch to join (20 sts).

Round 3: Ch2, * dc, (hdc, dc) in next stitch, repeat from * to complete round, sl st to first stitch to join (30 sts).

Round 4: Ch1, * sc, hdc, (dc, sc) in next stitch, repeat from * to complete round, sl st to first stitch to join (40 sts).

Round 5: Ch2, * dc, sc, hdc, sc repeat from * to complete round, sl st to first stitch to join.

Round 6: Ch1, * sc, dc, ch1, skip 1 stitch, dc in next stitch, hdc, repeat from * to complete round, sl st to first stitch to join.

Rounds 7–12: Repeat Rounds 5–6 three times.

Round 13: Join Color C, fasten off Color B, ch1, sc in blo of each stitch.

Rounds 14–17: Working continuously in the round, sc in each stitch.

To finish, sl st to first stitch of round to join. Fasten off. Weave in ends.

X-LARGE

Using Color B, ch4.

Round 1: 11dc in fourth chain from hook, sl st to first stitch to join round (11 sts).

Round 2: Ch1, (sc, dc) in each stitch, sl st to first stitch to join (22 sts).

Round 3: Ch2, * dc, (hdc, dc) in next stitch, repeat from * to complete round, sl st to first stitch to join (33 sts).

Round 4: Ch1, * sc, hdc, (dc, sc) in next stitch, repeat from * to complete round, sl st to first stitch to join (44 sts).

Round 5: Ch2, * dc, sc, hdc, sc repeat from * to complete round, sl st to first stitch to join.

Round 6: Ch1, * sc, dc, ch1, skip 1 stitch, dc in next stitch, repeat from * to complete round, sl st to first stitch to join.

Rounds 7–12: Repeat Rounds 4–5 three times.

Round 13: Join Color C, fasten off Color B, ch1, sc in blo of each stitch.

Rounds 14–18: Working continuously in the round, sc in each stitch.

To finish, sl st to first stitch of round to join. Fasten off. Weave in ends.

Finishing

Stack small button on top of large button with holes lined up. With sewing needle and thread, sew button stack onto hat.

How to Read My Patterns

Skill Level

To help you pick a pattern that is consistent with your crochet experience, every pattern in the book indicates its skill level: beginner, intermediate, or advanced. For patterns designated for beginners, you'll need to know how to chain, single crochet, half double crochet, and/or double crochet. As you move up the skill level ladder, more stitch knowledge is required, but there are photo tutorials included in this book for every single stitch you'll need to know. And none of the patterns are difficult. My design goal is always to create the sweetest items using the simplest stitches possible.

Sizing

Head sizes vary from person to person, and change with age from the time you are born until you fully mature. To crochet the right size hat, you need to know the circumference of the head it is intended for. Simply wrap a tape measure around the widest part of the head (over the hair) from the forehead, above the ears and around the back, then to the front again.

Each of the patterns contains directions for at least three sizes (Small, Medium, and Large) and, depending on the style of the hat, might also include directions for X-Small and/or X-Large. Here is how the measurements break down for the sizes (the age range for each size is approximate; pick the size to crochet based on head circumference):

- X-Small (0–3 months): 12–14.5"/30.5–37 cm
- Small (6–12 months): 15–17.5"/38–44.5 cm
- Medium (toddler to age 10): 17.5–19"/44.5–48 cm
- Large (teenager/adult woman): 19–22.5"/48–57 cm
- X-Large (adult man): 23–24.5"/58.5–62 cm

Yarn

Under Yarn, you will find listed the specific yarn(s) and colors I used to crochet the pattern, plus how many skeins you'll need. Also included is that specific yarn's "yarn weight." You'll find this information on the label of every skein of yarn you buy, and it ranges from #0 (lace weight) to #6 (super bulky weight). If you can't find the specific yarn I

use or you'd like to use something else, knowing the yarn weight will let you pick another yarn that will have the same gauge.

Hooks and Other Materials

Here you'll find the hook sizes you'll need, plus any additional materials or tools, which most commonly will include stitch markers, a yarn needle, and a sewing needle and thread.

Gauge

The key to crocheting a garment that fits is to check gauge. Every pattern in this book tells you the gauge for that project—the number of stitches and rows per inch the final measurements (and final fit) were based on.

To check gauge, you need to crochet a sample swatch using the yarn, hook size, and crochet stitch called for. Crochet the swatch at least 1"/2.5 cm larger than required so that you can check the stitches and rows within the swatch to ensure proper gauge. For instance, if the gauge given is a 3"/7.5 cm square in single crochet, you will work up a swatch in single crochet that is at least 4"/10 cm square. Lay a measuring tape on the swatch and count how many stitches you have in 3"/7.5 cm. Now reposition the tape and measure up and down to count how many rows you have in 3"/7.5 cm.

If you have more stitches and rows than you should, try the next larger hook size, and make another gauge swatch. Keep doing this until the swatch matches the pattern gauge. If you have fewer stitches and rows than you should, retest your gauge with the next size smaller hook in same way.

Notes

Be sure to read the Notes section before beginning a project. You'll find helpful hints there, including what stitches beyond the basic single crochet and double crochet might be used and cross-references to tutorials for them.

Special Techniques

A few of the patterns include stitch tutorials, which you'll find under Special Techniques. In most cases, these stitches are particular to that specific pattern.

Directions

- When a number is before the command, such as 3hdc, you will work the command in the SAME stitch.
- When a number is after the command, such as hdc3, you will work that command in that number of following stitches.
- The number in parentheses at the end of a round or row is the TOTAL number of stitches for that round or row.
- The asterisks will mark a specific placement in a pattern that will be used when repeating sections.
- Working "in the round" means that you will be working in one direction throughout, not back and forth in rows. To work "continuously in the round" means that the rounds will be crocheted in a spiral, without joining at the end of each round.
- When you see commands written within a set of parentheses, all those commands will be crocheted in the same stitch, for example "(ch1, dc, ch1) in the next stitch."

Abbreviations

blo	back loop only
bpdc	back post double crochet
bpsc	back post single crochet
ch	chain
dc	double crochet
dc dec	double crochet decrease
dec	decrease
dtr	double treble crochet
flo	front loop only
fpdc	front post double crochet
fpdc dec	front post double crochet decrease
fpsc	front post single crochet
fptr	front post treble crochet
hdc	half double crochet
hdc dec	half double crochet decrease
inc	increase
rev sc	reverse single crochet
sc	single crochet
sc dec	single crochet decrease
sk	skip
sl st	slip stitch
sl st dec	slip stitch decrease
st(s)	stitch(es)
tr	treble crochet

Standard Yarn Weight System

Categories of yarn, gauge ranges, and recommended needle and hook sizes

Yarn Weight Symbol & Category Names	0 LACE	1 SUPER FINE	2 FINE	3 LIGHT	4 MEDIUM	5 BULKY	6 SUPER BULKY
Type of Yarns in Category	Fingering 10-count crochet thread	Sock, Fingering, Baby	Sport, Baby	DK, Light Worsted	Worsted, Afghan, Aran	Chunky, Craft, Rug	Bulky, Roving
Knit Gauge Range* in Stockinette Stitch to 4 inches	33–40** sts	27–32 sts	23–26 sts	21–24 st	16–20 sts	12–15 sts	6–11 sts
Recommended Needle in Metric Size Range	1.5–2.25 mm	2.25–3.25 mm	3.25–3.75 mm	3.75–4.5 mm	4.5–5.5 mm	5.5–8 mm	8 mm and larger
Recommended Needle U.S. Size Range	000–1	1 to 3	3 to 5	5 to 7	7 to 9	9 to 11	11 and larger
Crochet Gauge* Ranges in Single Crochet to 4 inch	32–42 double crochets**	21–32 sts	16–20 sts	12–17 sts	11–14 sts	8–11 sts	5–9 sts
Recommended Hook in Metric Size Range	Steel*** 1.6–1.4 mm	2.25–3.5 mm	3.5–4.5 mm	4.5–5.5 mm	5.5–6.5 mm	6.5–9 mm	9 mm and larger
Recommended Hook U.S. Size Range	Steel*** 6, 7, 8 Regular hook B–1	B–1 to E–4	E–4 to 7	7 to I–9	I–9 to K–10 1/2	K–10 1/2 to M–13	M–13 and larger

* GUIDELINES ONLY: The above reflect the most commonly used gauges and needle or hook sizes for specific yarn categories.

** Lace weight yarns are usually knitted or crocheted on larger needles and hooks to create lacy, openwork patterns. Accordingly, a gauge range is difficult to determine. Always follow the gauge stated in your pattern.

*** Steel crochet hooks are sized differently from regular hooks—the higher the number, the smaller the hook, which is the reverse of regular hook sizing.

Source: Craft Yarn Council of America's www.YarnStandards.com

Stitch Guide

H ere you will find everything you need to know to crochet the patterns in this book, even if you've never picked up a crochet hook before.

How to Hold a Crochet Hook

There are two ways to hold a hook; use the one that's most comfortable for you.

OVER THE HOOK HOLD

Place your hand over the hook with the handle resting against the palm and thumb and your index finger on the thumb rest.

UNDER THE HOOK HOLD

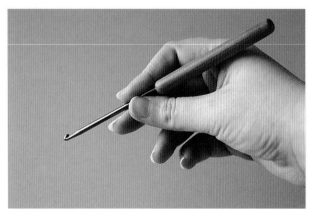

Hold the hook in your hand as you would hold a pencil between your thumb and forefinger.

How to Hold Yarn

Like holding the hook, there are several different ways to hold the yarn when crocheting. Choose the one that is most comfortable. Pay attention to tension, which is how tightly you are pulling on the yarn. You want to maintain an even tension, which will yield a fabric with evenly sized stitches, not too loose and not too tight.

OVER THE PINKIE HOLD

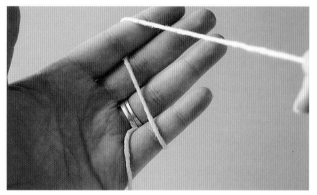

Wrap the yarn over your hand and around your pinky, then up and over your forefinger.

OVER THE MIDDLE FINGER HOLD

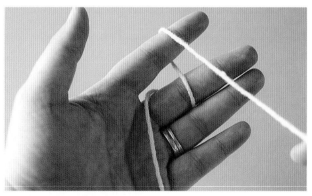

Wrap the yarn around your middle finger and over your forefinger to guide the yarn.

OVER THE FOREFINGER HOLD

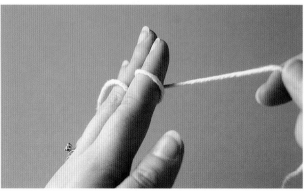

Wrap the yarn around your forefinger.

Slip Knot

Every crochet project will begin with this adjustable knot.

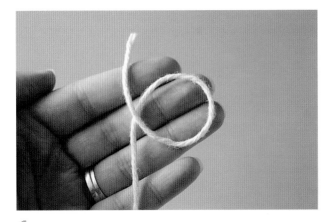

1 Make a loop in the yarn.

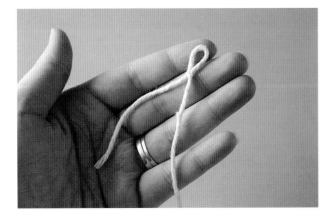

2 With your crochet hook or finger, grab the yarn from the skein and pull it through the loop.

3 Pull tight on the yarn and adjust to create first loop.

Chain (ch)

The chain provides the foundation for your stitches at the beginning of a pattern. It can also serve as a stitch within a pattern and can be used to create an open effect.

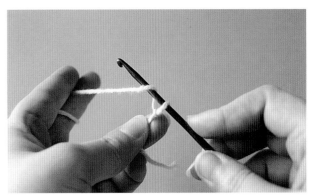

1 Insert the hook through the slip knot and "yarn over" by bringing the hook up under the yarn.

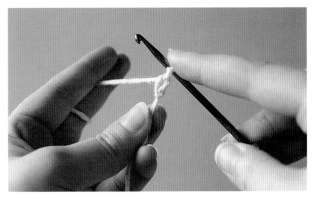

2 Keeping the yarn taut (but not too tight; see Tip below), pull the hook back through the loop, bringing the yarn with it. Chain 1 is complete.

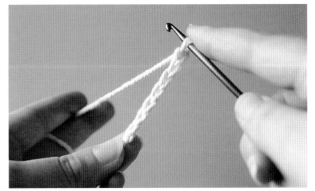

3 Repeat Steps 1 and 2 to create multiple chains.

TIP Keep chains loose to ensure consistency and make it easier to work the following stitches.

Anatomy of a Stitch

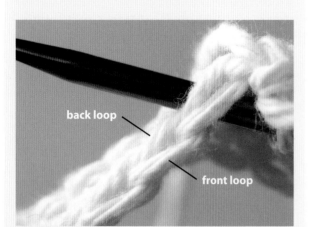

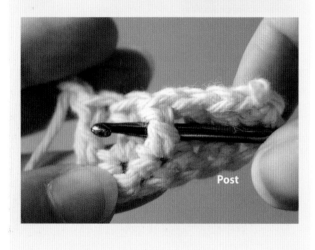

Crocheting into a Stitch

Unless otherwise instructed, you will insert your hook under both loops to crochet any stitch.

CROCHETING INTO THE FRONT OR BACK OF A STITCH

At times you will be instructed to work through the front loop only (flo) or the back loop only (blo) of a stitch to create a texture within the pattern.

Inserting hook to crochet into the front loop only (flo) of a stitch

Inserting hook to crochet into the back loop only (blo) of a stitch

Slip Stitch (sl st)

The slip stitch is used to join one stitch to another or to join a stitch to another point.

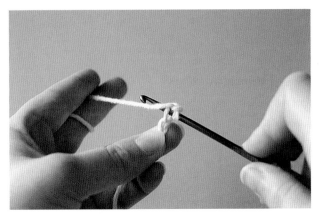

1 Insert the hook from the front of the stitch to the back of stitch and yarn over, just as for a chain stitch.

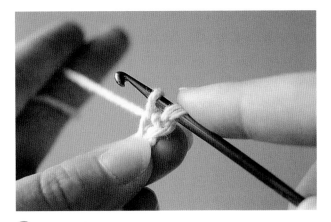

2 Pull the yarn back through the stitch: 2 loops on hook.

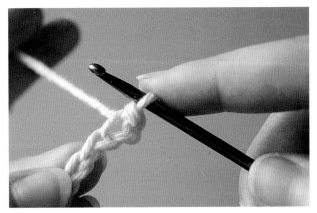

3 Continue to pull the loop that you just pulled up through the original loop on the hook to finish.

Single Crochet (sc)

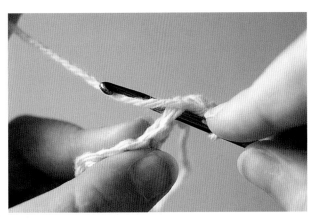

1 Insert the hook from the front of the stitch to the back and yarn over.

2 Pull the yarn back through the stitch: 2 loops on hook.

3 Yarn over and draw the yarn through both loops on the hook to complete the stitch.

Single Crochet Decrease (sc dec)

A single crochet decrease will take two stitches and make them into one single crochet stitch.

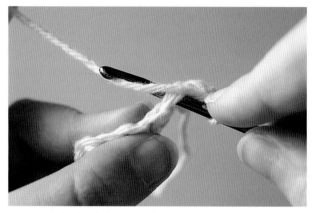

1 Insert the hook from the front of the stitch to the back and yarn over.

2 Pull the yarn back through the stitch: 2 loops on hook.

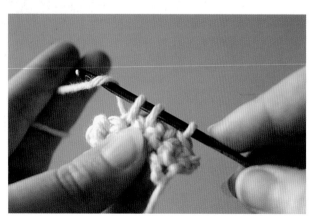

3 Leaving the loops on the hook, insert the hook front to back into the next stitch. Yarn over and pull yarn back through stitch: 3 loops on hook.

4 Yarn over and draw yarn through all 3 loops on the hook to complete the stitch.

Half Double Crochet (hdc)

1 Yarn over and insert the hook from the front of the stitch to the back.

2 Yarn over and pull the yarn back through the stitch: 3 loops on hook.

3 Yarn over and draw yarn through all 3 loops on the hook to complete the stitch.

Half Double Crochet Decrease (hdc dec)

1 Yarn over and insert the hook from the front of the stitch to the back.

2 Yarn over and pull the yarn back through the stitch: 3 loops on hook.

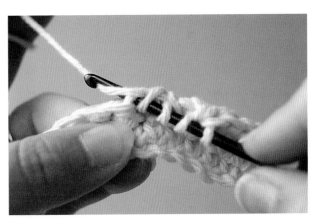

3 Yarn over and insert the hook front to back into the next stitch.

4 Yarn over and pull the yarn back through the stitch: 5 loops on hook.

5 Yarn over and pull the yarn through all 5 loops on the hook to complete the stitch.

Double Crochet (dc)

1 Yarn over and insert the hook from the front of the stitch to the back.

2 Yarn over and pull the yarn back through the stitch: 3 loops on hook.

3 Yarn over and draw the yarn through the first 2 loops on the hook: 2 loops on hook.

4 Yarn over and draw the yarn through the remaining 2 loops on the hook to complete the stitch.

Double Crochet Decrease (dc dec)

A double crochet decrease will take two stitches and make them into one double crochet stitch.

1 Yarn over and insert the hook from the front of the stitch to the back.

2 Yarn over and pull the yarn back through the stitch: 3 loops on hook.

3 Yarn over and draw the yarn through the first 2 loops on the hook: 2 loops on hook.

4 Leaving the loops on the hook, insert the hook front to back into the next stitch. Yarn over and pull the yarn back through the stitch: 4 loops on hook.

5 Yarn over and draw the yarn through the first 2 loops on the hook: 3 loops on hook.

6 Yarn over and draw the yarn through all 3 loops on the hook to complete the stitch.

Front Post Double Crochet (fpdc)

1 Yarn over and insert the hook around the post of the stitch from the front to the back to the front of the work (see Anatomy of a Stitch on page 124 for where the post is located).

2 Yarn over and pull the yarn back around the post: 3 loops on hook.

(continued)

3 Yarn over and draw the yarn through the first 2 loops on the hook: 2 loops on hook.

2 Yarn over and pull the yarn back around the post: 3 loops on hook.

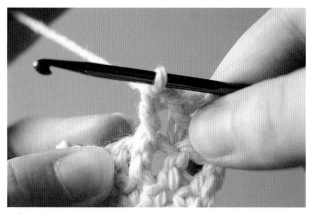

4 Yarn over and draw the yarn through the remaining 2 loops on the hook to complete the stitch.

3 Yarn over and draw the yarn through the first 2 loops on the hook: 2 loops on hook.

Back Post Double Crochet (bpdc)

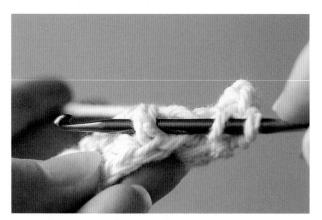

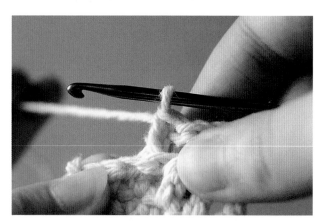

4 Yarn over and draw the yarn through the remaining 2 loops on the hook to complete the stitch.

1 Yarn over and insert the hook around the post of the stitch from the back to the front to the back of the work (see Anatomy of a Stitch on page 124 for where the post is located). The photo shows the back of the stitch.

Treble Crochet (tr)

1 Yarn over 2 times and insert the hook from the front of the stitch to the back.

2 Yarn over and pull the yarn back through the stitch: 4 loops on hook.

3 Yarn over and draw the yarn through the first 2 loops on the hook: 3 loops on hook.

4 Yarn over and draw the yarn through the next 2 loops on the hook: 2 loops on hook.

5 Yarn over and draw the yarn through the last 2 loops on the hook to complete the stitch.

Changing Colors

When switching yarns in a piece, use this technique for a clean color change.

1 For a single crochet: Insert the hook through the last stitch before the color change and pull the yarn back through the stitch.

(continued)

2 Yarn over with the NEXT color and pull through. The color change is complete. Cut the yarn for the original color.

If you are working a color change for a half double crochet, double crochet, or triple crochet, complete the stitch until the last pull through. Yarn over with the NEXT color and pull through to complete the color change.

3 To change colors again, insert the hook through the next stitch and pull the yarn back through the stitch.

Carrying Yarn

In patterns where you are switching back and forth between colors multiple times, you may be instructed to drop one yarn and pick up another instead of fastening off the original color. This is called carrying a yarn and it allows you to simply pick the yarn up later, with no ends to weave in. When you carry a yarn or yarns, it's very important to maintain an even tension when you pick up the carried yarn. If the yarn is carried too tightly, your fabric will pucker; if carried too loosely, the stitches can enlarge.

To carry a color, follows Steps 1 and 2 of Changing Colors. Do not cut the yarn when the color change is complete.

4 Drop the current color, yarn over with the color you are carrying, and pull through.

The color change is complete. Continue with the new color, carrying the old one behind the work and repeating Steps 3 and 4 when you need to change colors again.

Finishing Touches

Here we cover everything you need for a beautiful finish to your project, from seams to embellishments.

Fastening Off

When you reach the end of your crochet project, you will need to fasten off the yarn. To fasten off simply means to cut the yarn and secure the end.

To fasten off, cut the yarn, leaving a few inches (unless otherwise instructed), and draw the end of the yarn through the last loop on your hook. Pull tight to secure.

Weaving in Ends

1 Use your hook or a yarn needle to weave any cut ends up and down through 3 to 4 stitches. I also add a slip stitch to help secure the ends.

2 After weaving it, trim the end as close to the garment as possible to hide it.

Pom-Pom

1 Wrap yarn around a large glass or piece of cardboard (approximately 6"/15 cm wide) 40 times (or more if you want the pom-pom to be thicker).

2 Carefully remove the yarn from the glass or cardboard. Holding the hank of yarn closed in one hand, tie a short length of yarn tightly around the hank in the middle and knot or slip knot it 2 or 3 times (shown in contrasting color).

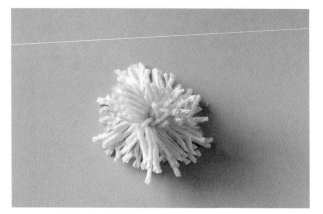

3 Cut the hank open at each end and trim evenly. Secure the pom-pom to the item by slipping a long piece of yarn through the yarn tied around the center and knotting it securely to the item.

4 Fluff the pom-pom to finish.

Sewing Stitches

In many of these patterns, you will need to sew on an embellishment like a flower or eyes, or sew two pieces of a garment together. Here are two stitches I often use, worked in a contrasting color so that you can see how they are done.

WHIPSTITCH

1 Hold the right sides of the items together and, using your needle, go under both sets of stitches. Repeat, always coming in from the same side and going out on the opposite side.

This is what the stitches will look like right sides facing out.

RUNNING STITCH

1 Hold the right sides of the pieces together and go
under the first 2 sets of stitches. Do not go over the
stitches.

2 Turn the needle and go back under the NEXT set of
stitches. You will be working around the posts of the
stitches.

*As you work running stitch, notice that you're working around
the posts and NOT over the stitches.*

This is what the stitches will look like right sides facing out.

Sewing Embellishments

When adding an embellishment (like a nose or eyes) to a
hat, simply sew it on with the yarn needle as shown.

1 Hold the piece on top of the garment and insert the
yarn needle through both pieces from the back to front,
sewing through the last row of the embellishment.

2 Continue to sew around the piece until the edge is
secure. Fasten off. Weave in ends.

Visual Index

Mary Kate
Cloche 2

Downtown
Girl Slouchy 22

Horse Hat ... 6

Rosey
Newsboy 24

Giggle
Monster 10

Giggles and
Curls Hat 28

Ahoy Matey!
Pirate Hat 14

Baby Doll
Hat 32

Bubblegum
Machine
Beanie 18

Zack the
Zombie 36

Twisted Stitches Beanie 40

Daddy's Bearded Dude Beanie 60

I'm an Elf! Pixie 44

Luvbug Slouchy 64

Sock Monkey Twist 48

Sweetheart Sunhat 68

Groovy Waves Beanie 52

Lamb Bonnet 72

Ocean Air Cloche 56

Just Like Mommy Ribbed Beanie 76

Basketweave Beanie 80

You Have My Heart Beanie 100

Buddy Bobbles 84

Snowman Hat 104

Winter Lodge Hat 88

Gone Huntin' Camo Cap 108

Hooded Scarf 92

Pigtail Hat 112

Sassy Girl 96

Thick and Thin Hat 116